"Stuart Briscoe shows that effective leadership is not 'what you know', it's 'Who you know'. And to be a Christian leader, you must be *Brave Enough to Follow*. Every emerging leader must learn to embrace this paradox."

— MARSHALL SHELLEY
editor, *Leadership Magazine*,
www.christianitytoday.com

"*Brave Enough to Follow* is vintage Briscoe — insightful, challenging, uplifting and inspirational. This book is a great encouragement for anyone who feels they have nothing to offer to Jesus. I heartily recommend it."

— BISHOP FRANK RETIEF
presiding bishop of the Church of England in South Africa

"Stuart Briscoe belongs to a most influential group of Christian authors who strengthens leaders of the Body of Christ worldwide. I struggled to distance myself from the Apostle Peter's life in *Brave Enough to Follow* only to joyfully succumb to the clarity, simplicity, and honesty of an experienced pastor treating an archetypal subject."

— RAMESH RICHARD PH.D., TH.D.
president, *RREACH* International; professor, Dallas Theological Seminary

"This book is filled with practical insights on spiritual formation. Here is a 'coach's manual on leadership formation,' helping us see the grace-filled pattern of the Master."

— J. PAUL LANDREY
international director of TOPIC
(Trainers of Pastors International Coalition)

"The life of Peter demonstrates that we can never be too weak for God — but we can be too strong for him. Stuart Briscoe with all his warmth, wit, and wisdom encourages us in our journey with Jesus to muster the bravery to begin, the courage to continue, and the faith to finish knowing it is more about our availability to God than our ability for God."

— Charles Price
senior pastor, The Peoples Church, Toronto, Canada

"Stuart Briscoe believes in using sanctified imagination to unlock biblical narratives. This captivating book is the result. It gives new eyes to perceive old truths. I highly recommend it."

— Rev. Edmund Chan
senior pastor, Covenant EFC (Singapore); author, *Growing Deep in God*

STUART BRISCOE

BRAVE ENOUGH *to* FOLLOW

WHAT JESUS CAN DO WHEN YOU KEEP YOUR EYES ON HIM

A 10-WEEK WALK WITH JESUS AND SIMON PETER

NAVPRESS®

BRINGING TRUTH TO LIFE

OUR GUARANTEE TO YOU

We believe so strongly in the message of our books that we are making this quality guarantee to you. If for any reason you are disappointed with the content of this book, return the title page to us with your name and address and we will refund to you the list price of the book. To help us serve you better, please briefly describe why you were disappointed. Mail your refund request to: NavPress, P.O. Box 35002, Colorado Springs, CO 80935.

The Navigators is an international Christian organization. Our mission is to reach, disciple, and equip people to know Christ and to make Him known through successive generations. We envision multitudes of diverse people in the United States and every other nation who have a passionate love for Christ, live a lifestyle of sharing Christ's love, and multiply spiritual laborers among those without Christ.

NavPress is the publishing ministry of The Navigators. NavPress publications help believers learn biblical truth and apply what they learn to their lives and ministries. Our mission is to stimulate spiritual formation among our readers.

Published in association with the literary agency of Alive Communications, Inc. 7680 Goddard Street, Suite 200, Colorado Springs, Colorado, 80920

ISBN 1-57683-592-8

Cover design by Chris Gilbert
Cover photo by Steve Gardner / His Image Pixelworks
Creative Team: Greg Clouse, Rachelle Gardner, Arvid Wallen, Darla Hightower, Glynese Northam

Some of the anecdotal illustrations in this book are true to life and are included with the permission of the persons involved. All other illustrations are composites of real situations, and any resemblance to people living or dead is coincidental.

Unless otherwise identified, all Scripture quotations in this publication are taken from the HOLY BIBLE: NEW INTERNATIONAL VERSION® (NIV®). Copyright © 1973, 1978, 1984 by International Bible Society. Used by permission of Zondervan Publishing House. All rights reserved. Other versions used include: THE MESSAGE (MSG). Copyright © 1993, 1994, 1995, 1996, 2000, 2001, 2002. Used by permission of NavPress Publishing Group.

Briscoe, D. Stuart.
  Brave enough to follow : what Jesus can do when you keep your eyes on him : a 10-week walk with Jesus and Simon Peter / Stuart Briscoe.
    p. cm.
  Includes bibliographical references (p.   ).
  ISBN 1-57683-592-8
  1. Peter, the Apostle, Saint. 2. Christian leadership--Biblical teaching. 3. Bible. N.T. Gospels--Criticism, interpretation, etc. I. Title.
  BS2515.B736 2004
  225.9'2--dc22

                         2004002805

Printed in the United States of America
1 2 3 4 5 6 7 8 9 10 / 08 07 06 05 04

FOR A FREE CATALOG OF NAVPRESS BOOKS & BIBLE STUDIES,
CALL 1-800-366-7788 (USA) OR 1-416-499-4615 (CANADA)

To my three adult children,
David, Judy, and Pete,
all of whom bring their Dad great joy because
they are brave enough to follow Jesus.

TABLE OF CONTENTS

ACKNOWLEDGMENTS

A couple of years ago I was invited to speak to a representative group of church leaders from Latin America in Quito, Ecuador, under the auspices of T.O.P.I.C (Training of Pastors International Coalition). The conference was called to discuss ways that thousands of church leaders who have no formal theological education — and no chance of getting any — might receive some kind of informal training. During my sessions, I addressed the scriptural account of Peter and John standing before the Sanhedrin, speaking powerfully about the Lord. These two disciples impressed upon their inquisitors that, despite their lack of formal training, they were extremely effective, and the reason was that "they had been with Jesus." Many of us went away from that conference pondering what it means for both trained and untrained men and women to be like Peter and John, spending their lives "being with Jesus" and following him!

Some of the Spanish-speaking church leaders asked me if the material could be made available for the Spanish church, so I decided to write it — in English!—and they promised to translate and publish it. I started to work, and it then occurred to me that as the manuscript was already in English, an American publisher might be interested in it. At this point my agent, Andrea Christian from Alive Communications, stepped forward and used her considerable skill to arrange for publication by NavPress.

At this juncture another gifted young woman, Rachelle Gardner, appeared on the scene and promptly became, in addition to my editor, something resembling the chief cheerleader for the book. She suggested that my original title, "The Unlikely Leader," might convey the impression that this was a leadership book, when it is actually about both "follow-ship" and leadership, and we agreed the title should reflect this. In addition, she worked hard crafting the discussion questions that have made the book suitable for far more people than I first envisioned. So, many thanks to NavPress, Andrea Christian, and Rachelle Gardner.

I also gladly acknowledge the help I received from two old classics, namely Graham Scroggie's *A Guide to the Gospels* and Alexander Bruce's *The Training of the Twelve,* although any errors that have survived the editorial process, and my occasional flights of fancy (which I suspect may not have met with their approval) are my responsibility and mine alone.

It is customary for authors to thank their patient wives who have cheerfully borne the inattention of their author husbands during the long hours of writing. This I would gladly do, if it were not for the fact that my wife, Jill, has been so busy writing her own books and meeting deadlines that she has found my inattention a great blessing.

UNSCHOOLED, ORDINARY MEN

When they saw the courage of Peter and John and realized that
they were unschooled, ordinary men, they were astonished and
they took note that these men had been with Jesus.

ACTS 4:13

Near the Temple in Jerusalem, the Great Sanhedrin was in
session. As the high court of Israel, this group of formidable politicians was responsible for judging the civic and religious
issues of the day on the basis of Jewish law. Simon Peter and John
stood before a semi-circle of seventy inquisitors, facing open hostil-
ity. The members of the Sanhedrin were infuriated that Peter and
John had performed a spectacular miracle, healing a crippled man,
and had been preaching a powerful message to the crowds about
Jesus rising from the dead. *These wretched followers of Jesus were becoming
more and more credible.* Thousands were being persuaded. It was a
major threat to the Sanhedrin's power.

The interrogation began. Referring to the miraculous healing of
the cripple, members of the Sanhedrin asked imperiously, "By what
power or what name did you do this?" After a respectful acknowledgment of the prestigious company before whom he was standing,
Peter made a comment dripping with irony. "If we are being called

to account today for an act of kindness . . ." In other words, *if we are being charged with the heinous crime of meeting a need, being generous and caring* . . . Then Peter went on to give a bold, uncompromising answer to their question. "It is by the name of Jesus Christ of Nazareth, whom you crucified but whom God raised from the dead." There it was — a direct indictment. Discretion might have required that Peter be more respectful. After all, these men could eliminate him at any moment. But Peter was in no mood for playing it safe. He wanted this distinguished body to know they were complicit in the murder of an innocent man. More than that — this man was none other than the Messiah.

The members of the Sanhedrin "couldn't take their eyes off them — Peter and John standing there so confident, so sure of themselves! Their fascination deepened when they realized these two were laymen with no training in Scripture or formal education" (Acts 4:13, MSG). No doubt these powerful men were taken aback that Peter and John completely flouted traditional Sanhedrin protocol, which demanded that persons brought before them should be dressed in mourning and appear humble in attitude. Peter was an unvarnished, straight-shooting rugged fisherman, unabashed and unashamed — and not exactly the picture of humility.

How could such a man — this nobody out of nowhere — take such a bold stance? Peter had deserted his Teacher at the time of his crucifixion — evidence of cowardice and an indictment on the credibility of Jesus himself. Yet, now Peter stood in the presence of the most powerful religious men in the land, and he was speaking with power, conviction, and a reckless disregard for his own well-being. The rulers, elders, and teachers of the law "were astonished."

It dawned on the members of the Sanhedrin, "these men had been with Jesus." That must have been the source of their transformation. John and Peter were desperately ordinary, but Jesus had made them capable of extraordinary feats. Yes, they had followed Jesus alright. And He had rubbed off on them, big time.

Simon Peter went on to become one of the greatest leaders the church has ever known, but if you had seen where he came from, you wouldn't have believed it possible. He was not known to be the most courageous of men. He was a humble fisherman, working with his hands, supporting his family, and enjoying the camaraderie of his family and good friends, fellow fisherman. His three years with Jesus would be marked by notable failures, particularly in the area of courage. Simply put, Peter may not have been brave enough to be the leader he was destined to become. But Jesus knew that Peter *was* brave enough to follow him — and that was all that mattered.

We often fall under the misconception that for God to do great work through us, we need to have "the makings" of greatness — a certain boldness, the guts to get up in front of people and take charge. But (as is often the case when we study God's way of doing things) the reality is upside down from what we think it should be. We don't have to have the courage to lead; we just need to be brave enough to follow. When we follow him, Christ will make us into what He intends for us to be.

The history of great men in the Bible reveals that Simon Peter was just one in a long line of very unlikely leaders, chosen by God to play a pivotal role in bringing people to his kingdom. Abraham, Moses, David, Joseph — all were improbable choices for one reason or another. Some exhibited classic bravery as leaders; others did not. But they all had one major feature in common: They would commit to following the Lord their God. Soon, another unlikely disciple would join the scene — Saul of Tarsus, whose commitment to "following" transformed him into the great apostle Paul.

Why does Jesus choose to do his work through such seemingly unlikely people?

When the Sanhedrin responded to Peter's testimony by saying, "these men had been with Jesus," they were playing right into God's hand. By choosing to work through ordinary people — with obvious flaws and frailties — God ensures that when something powerful happens, *He alone will get the glory.* God's power always shines through, but it is especially apparent to others when a formerly gutless person appears suddenly bold. The Sanhedrin, who rejected Jesus, were unwittingly glorifying him by acknowledging him as the source of surprising, transforming power.

In fact, it seems the more powerless the leader, the more glory God receives. And He delights in this! Remember Gideon? A hesitant and fearful man, God nevertheless chose him to lead Israel in defeating the formidable Midianites, who dominated Israel at the time. Not only did God choose Gideon, He gave Gideon an army of only three hundred men to conquer the Midianite army of 32,000. Gideon seemed like the absolute wrong choice for the job — he was so fearful that he kept demanding miraculous proof that God was with him. But the key to understanding this choice is the fact that, once Gideon was clear *Who* was leading, he was able to muster the courage to obey. He never thought of himself as a leader. He simply had to follow. God made it clear that his decision to handle the Midianites in this manner was so that, when the Israelites were triumphant, He and He alone would get the glory.

Jeremiah 9:23 says, "Let not the wise man boast of his wisdom or the strong man boast of his strength or the rich man boast of his riches, but let him who boasts, boast about this: that he understands and knows me, that I am the LORD." In other words, if God always chose the obvious leaders to do his work, people would take all the glory for themselves. But if we are clearly weak and flawed, yet we have a part in establishing his kingdom, we cannot boast about ourselves but must instead boast that we know the Lord. God does great things through the not-so-brave among us, so the world can see that the glory is his and his alone. Paul reiterates this idea in 1 Corinthians 1:26-31, where he talks about how God chose the foolish, weak, and lowly among us to do his work, "so that no one may boast before him" (verse 29).

Right about now you may be wondering, *What does all this have to do with me?* Well you, my friend, just might have been thinking you'll never be significant in God's kingdom. I want you to know that all it takes for you to become everything that God intends for you is a willingness — yes, the bravery — to follow him. Jesus knows you. He has identified you in the lineup. He has called you to be part of his kingdom, and the role you will play, no matter how apparently small, is a crucial part of his vast plan for all of us.

Jesus knows your hidden potential. Gideon had an invisible potential to be a great warrior. Moses had the unknown potential to steer thousands of pilgrims across a barren desert. Simon Peter had an unseen potential for powerful evangelism. You may have been given a glimpse of your own potential, or you may be completely in the dark. Either way, Jesus knows your potential, and if you follow him, He will transform you — and you will glorify him.

But how does Jesus transform someone from ordinary to significant? How does God take that unseen potential He plants in all of us and develop it so that we reflect his image to the world?

Jesus transforms each of us, not when we summon up the courage to be leaders, but when we commit to following him. He invites us to become deeply acquainted with him. When we seek him, He gives us glimpses of himself and glimpses of our potential. He walks with us. He patiently draws out our courage. He encourages us, directs us, and challenges us. He asks questions and gives answers. He tests us and allows us to test him. Eventually our lives are transformed from mediocrity to maturity, and we become what He intended for us all along.

For three years Peter walked with Jesus, ate with him, and even climbed mountains with him. Peter's journey of transformation is well documented in the four Gospels. We are privy to the conversations, the flashes of triumph, and the moments of utter despair. We see Peter questioning Jesus, confronting him, praising him, and rejecting him. As I studied Peter's relationship with Jesus, I was amazed. Here, right in front of our eyes, is a blueprint for what Jesus can do when we keep our eyes on him. (Not to mention what happens in the moments we take our eyes *off* him!) In the story of Peter's walk with Jesus, we see all the components of a life-changing journey of transformation.

This amazing thought led me to look even more closely at the steps Peter took to follow Jesus. In the midst of my study of the biblical text, it came to me that we might best understand Peter's metamorphosis — and by extension, our own — if I were to recreate his story in narrative form, telling it in an informal style, at times almost like a novel. Therefore you will note that this book interweaves the gospel story with touches of (I hope) sanctified imagination and a dash of humor. There are times when I'll speculate about the disciple's frame of mind or emotional response to a situation — things that aren't overtly stated in Scripture, but that we can legitimately surmise. By attempting to place ourselves in Peter's circumstances and imagining his motives, thoughts, and feelings, perhaps we'll be closer to our goal of comprehending what happens when a real-life person like Simon Peter commits to following the Master.

At the top of each chapter, I've listed the Scriptures from which I've drawn the subsequent material. You may want to read these verses in your Bible to orient yourself to the material being discussed, but it's not necessary to your understanding. Each chapter closes with a section that draws some connections between Peter's journey and our own (Brave Enough to Think About It), with some suggestions for discussion and action (Brave Enough for Action).

I will attempt to trace the ups and downs, the ins and outs of Peter's three eventful years with Jesus. We'll follow him and see how his experience reflects our own. From his mistakes we'll learn what *not* to do; from his triumphs we'll be challenged to identify his secrets of success and draw from the same resources made available to him. By God's grace we'll learn the lessons he learned. By applying what we learn from Peter and submitting to the journey ourselves, we will each become exactly the people God intends us to be. Most importantly, the reason for the journey — the reason it matters that we follow Christ — is that God will be glorified. Our very lives will become a testament to his greatness. People will look at us and realize, "this person has been with Jesus."

I've been enriched and changed through this journey — and I hope you will be, too.

chapter 1

IT'S ALL ABOUT POTENTIAL

JOHN 1:29-42
LUKE 4:31—5:11

*F*ollowing one of his breathtaking performances, the world renowned pianist Ignace Paderewski was told by an admirer, "Maestro, you are a genius." He replied, "Genius? Perhaps. But before I was a genius, I was a drudge." He was referring to the many years spent in endless hours of practice, unnoticed and unheralded. He wanted to make clear that however much his talent appeared to be inborn, it nevertheless took a great deal of work to develop.

In our culture, we have the phenomenon of the "overnight sensation." Sports legends, movie stars, and popular music artists burst upon the scene out of nowhere. We are ignorant of the years they spent honing their skills, paying their dues, and waiting tables.

Before Peter strode center stage on the floor of the Sanhedrin chamber, he had spent his life in the relative obscurity of a Galilean fishing village. But it was his brief, life-transforming time in the company of the Master — paying his dues — that prepared him for that moment in the spotlight.

It all started one day in the deserts of Judea, close by the Jordan River. Peter, whose name at the time was Simon, was going about his business as a fisherman on the Sea of Galilee. His brother Andrew — his fishing partner — had apparently been missing in action for a few days. Suddenly, Andrew appeared and out of the blue told Simon, "We've found him! We've found the Messiah."

What? Simon might have wondered for a moment if his brother had spent a little too much time in the wine cellar. But I'm sure Andrew went on to explain all that had happened in the previous few days. He had been following a mysterious prophet called John the Baptist, who was creating a stir down by the river. Born into a priestly family, John had exchanged the prestigious life of a priest for the hazardous calling of a prophet. (It was hazardous because the people had a nasty habit of expressing disapproval by stoning the prophets.) John had embraced a ministry of hard-hitting, challenging, prophetic preaching. His pulpit was a barren hillside, his sanctuary a desert wasteland. But his message was loud and clear: "The kingdom we've all been talking about is about to burst upon us. The Promised One we've heard about from our earliest days is about to appear. It's time to get ready — and that means a total change of heart. It's repentance time. Time to humble yourselves in public and confess that your lives need cleansing and forgiving. Time to decide whom you will serve."

This was radical preaching. Amazingly, the people flocked to hear John the Baptist even though he was rude and unkempt. People of social standing were not usually referred to as a "generation of vipers," but this is precisely what he called some of them.

An unknown carpenter named Jesus had joined the crowds and moved among them unrecognized. One day Jesus approached and requested baptism by John. At first declining, John finally agreed to baptize Jesus, and a remarkable thing happened. The Father's voice from heaven boomed out a powerful statement of approval of Jesus. There was a stirring in the heavens and the invisible Spirit of God assumed the form of a dove, resting intentionally upon Jesus, pointing out that Jesus was indeed none other than the Son of God.

Andrew and an unnamed friend were somewhere in the crowd, listening to John's preaching. They were there when John pointed to Jesus and proclaimed the stunning news, "This is the Lamb of God who takes away the sin of the world." Everybody within the sound of John's voice understood what this meant. The sacrificial system of the time required a lamb to be offered as a substitutionary sacrifice on the Day of Atonement. To be told that there was a man in their midst who would become a sacrificial substitute for the sin of the world — that was mind-boggling.

Andrew and his friend heard, and they badly wanted to believe. They promptly followed Jesus, who invited them to where He was staying. It was late afternoon, but they spent time together, and during those minutes or hours — who knows?—something profound happened. The men became convinced beyond a doubt that Jesus was indeed the Messiah, the Lamb who would take away their sin.

So Andrew rushed to tell his brother Simon. The news must have resonated with Simon, because the two brothers immediately took off looking for Jesus. They finally approached him, only to be stopped in their tracks. As Jesus looked at Simon He said, "You are Simon, son of John. You will be called Cephas." The Greek equivalent of Cephas is *Petros,* which in English becomes "Peter." And the meaning of all those names is "Rock." So without introduction or preamble, without ever having laid eyes on Simon before, Jesus got right down to business and said in effect, "I know who you are, and I know what you're going to become. You're going to be a rock."

Notice how Jesus phrased his declaration: "You *are* Simon . . . you *will be* Cephas." Present tense, future tense. What is Jesus seeing in this man Simon? Potential. *You are one thing now, but you will be something else in the future.*

This encounter did not happen by accident. It was God at work, a divine appointment. It's important to recognize this because we need to be aware that God has his own perspective on our lives. He is looking at us, and He knows us in a way that no one else can know. Our friends and family and even our enemies have opinions about us, but the only accurate perception is God's. We need to be brought into the position where we're exposed to the divine perspective. Peter came face-to-face with the divine perspective on his life on the day that he met Jesus. But what exactly was it?

When Jesus lived in Palestine, names usually reflected the parents' hopes and aspirations for their children. When a new name was given, it usually spoke of an unmistakable change in character or direction. In Simon's case, when Jesus gave him a new name, it meant that Jesus had something special in mind for the fisherman. This man would become a *rock* in the plan of God for humanity.

It's interesting that we don't know how Simon reacted to his remarkable introduction to Jesus. He must have wondered what in the world this guy had in mind for him. But there is no doubt that when Jesus looked carefully at Simon, He saw right into the soul of the man and recognized something that others might never have noticed. He saw Simon's potential.

It takes a trained eye to see what others cannot see. It took a Michelangelo to look at a spoiled block of marble, on which others had worked to no avail, and "see" his famous statue, *David*. What others saw as a crude block of stone at worst, or an unmanageable project at best, Michelangelo envisioned as a figure of a young boy about to confront a giant. The fourteen-feet high masterpiece stands to this day in Florence, Italy, as a testimonial to the artist's skill and his eye for potential.

John tells us in his gospel that Jesus "did not need man's testimony about man, for he knew what was in a man" (John 2:25). But what did Jesus see in Simon that led him to rename him Peter — Rock? He saw exactly what Simon could become in his hands. In addition, He knew what it would take to get him from where he was to where he needed to be. There was a possibility, a potential for all manner of things to happen in Simon Peter's life. This is true of us all.

Let's think about the sheer potential wrapped up in any individual life. Look at an acorn. It's packed with potential. It is just a little nut, but if you put it in the right place, under the right circumstances, and hang around long enough, it can become an oak tree. We, even more than an acorn, are packed with potential. Of course, this potential can take different shapes and different forms. There are four key words that explain the way God views the potential in human beings: creation, fall, redemption, and glory.

CREATION

Every human being is created by God and is therefore of great value and significance. Unlike the rest of the created order, humans are created in the divine image, so we reflect the creative genius of God. We are invested with creative abilities which, when channeled correctly, produce blessing and bounty for the whole of humanity. What creative abilities did Peter have? He was a good fisherman, but beyond that, he may have been unaware of his God-given significance. The possibility of having a positive impact on the world was present, but hidden.

Because we are created, we have a vast potential for good.

FALL

After Creation came the Fall. This happened when humans decided we knew better than God, that we could function well independently. The result was certainly a degree of independence. Unfortunately, it was the kind of independence a ship experiences when it drifts from its anchor onto the rocks, or a teenager enjoys when he throws off the restraints of a loving home to end up disillusioned in a prodigal's pig pen. A person who throws off divine controls does not enter a spiritual vacuum called freedom, but rather a dominating environment fraught with evil. Peter would have moments in which he thought he knew better than Jesus, only to be severely reprimanded by the Master for his submission to the "things of men," rather than the "things of God" (Matthew 16:23).

Because we are fallen, we have a potential for evil.

REDEMPTION

The presence of the Son of God on earth speaks loudly of the fact that God is neither disinterested in the human condition, nor disengaged as far as a remedy is concerned. He sent his Son into the world to redeem the world. In New Testament times, the slave market was a familiar sight in many cities and towns. Wretched people who were regarded as pieces of property were stood up on blocks and traded like cattle. Occasionally, someone would take pity on a slave, pay the price to purchase them, and set them free. The word for this was "redemption." This word found its way into the New Testament to describe what happened when Jesus stepped into the slave market of human existence, where — at the cost of his own life — He purchased our freedom. If we acknowledge his goodness and accept his benevolent reign in our lives, we begin to discover that He frees us from fear, disillusionment, and despair and leads us into new vistas of hope. Peter's commitment to Christ allowed him to be redeemed even in the face of his own unworthiness, and a lifetime of incredible growth and significance followed.

Because we are redeemed, we have a thrilling potential for growth.

GLORY

Because Christ's work of redemption is designed not only to rescue us from the consequences of sin, but also to eventually remove us from its presence and finally deliver us from its power, there are dimensions of redemption that will not be fully realized until we make it to glory. The redeemed person is always looking to the future, to the time when Christ will return to complete the work of redemption, with a view to what we will ultimately become. We have a sense of anticipation that serves as a challenge to reach ever upward and onward, and that brings peace and comfort when life is hard. For we know that there will be a brighter day tomorrow, and one day we will be home in the presence of Christ. Late in his life Peter would write, "The God of all grace, who called you to his eternal glory in Christ, after you have suffered a little while, will himself restore you and make you strong, firm and steadfast" (1 Peter 5:10).

Because we are bound for glory, we have a potential for joyful significance.

If we want to be fully the people we were created to be, we've got to think in terms of our God-given potential. We must choose whether the horizons of our lives are to be determined by our own ambitions or if we're going to open ourselves up to discovering God's perspective on our lives.

Sad to say, so often we fail to do that. As a result, it may be that vast potentials lie latent within the human soul. It seems to me that we often settle for considerably less than God had in mind when He created us. After all, as King David said, we are "fearfully and wonderfully made" (Psalm 139:14). If that's true, we must have been made for some fearfully wonderful purpose. Do you have any idea of the magnitude of your potential? When Jesus made his startling declaration that changed Peter's name and his life, it was a beacon for us. The message is: Jesus knows the vast potential in all of us, even if we don't. He knows our ultimate purpose.

Like each and every one of us, Peter had a potential for good and evil, for growth and for significance — and it would all add up to his God-given purpose. What Peter had yet to discover was that he would have the responsibility of determining whether his potential would be fulfilled. If he followed Jesus and cooperated with him, he would realize his potential. If he chose not to, his potential would lie dormant. We will see that Peter's choice led him to fulfill a purpose far greater than anything he could have imagined. His decision to follow Jesus would be the turning point in his life, the beginning of the development of his true potential.

So the last we saw Peter, he was standing slightly bemused and confused before Jesus, who in one short moment had peered into his soul, looked into his future, and summarized his life by seeing his *potential* and declaring his *purpose*. "You are Simon son of John. You will be called Cephas." Afterward, as Peter and Andrew made their way home along the banks of the Jordan, their minds were no doubt buzzing as they processed the dramatic encounter with Jesus. But on arriving home, things settled down, life returned to normal, and they took up their old routine of fishing in the beautiful Lake Gennesaret (the Sea of Galilee), trading their catch, and washing their nets. Until one day, after an amazing miracle at the local synagogue, Jesus happened to stop by Peter's house, where Peter's mother-in-law was suffering from a fever. He immediately healed her, and following this miraculous display, He was swamped with needy people who cried out to him for help and comfort. I can just picture Peter standing by in quiet awe. *Maybe He really is the Messiah.*

After leaving Galilee for a time, Jesus returned and was again besieged by a mob who hung on his every word. They crowded around him to such an extent that He was in danger of being pushed into the lake. Peter was nearby washing his nets. Jesus climbed into Peter's boat, and asked him to put out a short distance. Then Jesus sat down in the boat and spoke to the crowds who listened intently from the shore, while Peter quietly handled the oars, keeping the boat close to the people.

In some ways Jesus sounded like John the Baptist. He was announcing the arrival of a new kingdom, challenging the people to repent and to prepare their hearts and minds for the changes that God was about to bring in their lives. There was certainly a stir in the air, a sense that something was about to happen, not unlike an oncoming storm foreshadowed by subtle changes in weather that Peter had learned to read so well. But while Jesus' teaching seemed full of truth, it was also full of grace. There was no lack of power in what He said, and there was a winsomeness in the way He said it. His words must have sunk into Peter's soul while his mind kept drifting back to Jesus' enigmatic statement: "You are Simon — you will be

Peter." *What does it mean? What am I supposed to do?* For now, all Peter knew was that for some reason, he was beginning to trust this Jesus.

"Put out into the deep water and let down the nets for a catch," he heard Jesus say one day.

Now at that particular moment, putting out his nets was the last thing Peter was inclined to do. He'd spent a cold and frustrating night on the lake and caught nothing. And now he had just spent a good bit of time cleaning his precious nets. He had no intention of setting sail or getting his nets wet again, and he said so. But there was something about the way Jesus spoke to him that compelled Peter to add — perhaps to his own surprise — "But because you say so, I will let down the net." His fisherman's instincts told him that if the fish were not around in the cool of the night, they would not be there in the heat of the day. His practical nature insisted that to put carefully cleaned nets back into the water was a waste of time and effort. Moreover, strong-willed and opinionated men — and Peter was certainly both — don't like to be told what to do. So just for a fleeting second there was a clash of wills. But this time Peter yielded, heading out from shore.

I have often pondered what made Peter acquiesce in such an uncharacteristic way. Peter had no way of knowing that for the rest of his life he would encounter "because you say so" days. They're the days when everything inside you says, "This is *not* the way to go." Everything except the still, small voice of the Spirit who says, "Oh, yes, it is." You find yourself going where you had no intention of going, doing what you don't want to do, for no other reason than

Jesus said you should. It is the inner recognition that Jesus is right, that his word is truth, that his authority supercedes everything else. This was Peter's first experience of submitting himself to Christ's authority — and it wouldn't be the last. *"Because you say so,"* Peter muttered to himself, pulling on the oars. *But why am I doing this?* He was perplexed as he maneuvered past the other boats. I can just imagine how he recoiled at the thought of washing the nets all over again.

But Peter went ahead and let down his nets, shaking his head the entire time. *This is ridiculous.* Except for one thing — the water was alive with activity, boiling with motion. The fish were leaping and jumping and hurling themselves into the nets. *Where had they come from? Where had they been all night?*

Peter didn't have time to think. His nets were breaking. His livelihood was about to be ripped to shreds. He pulled and strained and hauled in the nets. The catch was phenomenal. His boat was sinking under the load.

"Help!" he shouted to his friends in a boat nearby. The other men must have wondered why Peter was fishing at that time, but what they saw blew their minds. He was being swamped by a catch of fish like they had never seen. They brought their boat alongside and began helping with the nets. Soon both boats were besieged with fish and beginning to sink.

Jesus seemed quite unfazed. This compelling man seemed to have power over men and demons and even fish. He was so quietly awesome that Peter, who was not easily overwhelmed, forgot about the sinking boats and the catch of a lifetime and fell on his knees among the tangled nets and the leaping fish. He shouted, "Go away from me, Lord; I am a sinful man."

This was a cry from the heart. A heart that was as confused and tangled as the shredded nets full of struggling fish — a heart not unlike our own. Peter knew there was plenty of need for repentance in his life. The promise of the kingdom of which Jesus spoke was both exciting and troubling, but definitely not deserved. The presence of Jesus in his life was at the same time endearing and condemning, comforting and disturbing. Something inside Peter longed to stay by Jesus' side, while something else screamed, "I've got to get away!" He was torn.

How do we cope with our own devastating imperfection in the presence of Jesus' perfection? How does our own mediocrity stand up to Jesus' superiority? Peter could not compete with such mastery and magnificence, and he was far from understanding that he didn't have to. He felt small and dirty, inadequate and petty, and he didn't know how to handle it.

"Lord," he said, and what he meant by his choice of title we cannot be sure, but from the depths of his soul he asked the Lord to leave him. Peter knew that if Jesus left, he would be desolate, but if He stayed, Peter would live with constant reminders of his own failures and shortcomings.

But Jesus wasn't going anywhere. He had work to do, and Peter was a major part of it. Jesus was not leaving, for the journey of a lifetime was about to begin.

Later in his life, Peter wrote, "Humble yourselves, therefore, under

God's mighty hand, that he may lift you up in due time" (1 Peter 5:6). That moment in the boat, with his inadequacies revealed, must have been the first of many humbling occasions in Peter's journey with Jesus. But isn't it interesting to note that the process of Peter's humbling had *not* begun by Jesus browbeating him about his failings, but by simply allowing Peter to see himself in comparison to Jesus?

We can always feel better by comparing ourselves to people whom we think are worse than us. The problem is that we often take the illogical step of assuming that because somebody is worse than us, we are alright. When we compare our lives to that of Jesus, we see ourselves like Peter did: as failing, fallen people, desperately in need of transformation. Until we see the extent of our frailness, it is unlikely that we'll seek anything that will change our lives and move us along the path toward realized potential. Comparing ourselves to Jesus is the surefire path to humility, and until we are humbled, God cannot lift us up. At this moment in the boat, Jesus began to change Peter's life. The moment of humility, the moment of recognition of our own unworthiness in the face of his awesome power, is the first moment of our transformation.

Peter had now encountered Jesus twice. The first time, when Jesus gave him a new name, he realized Jesus knew all about the potential in him. The second encounter (in the boat) gave Peter a fuller recognition of who Jesus Christ really is, which immediately gave Peter a deeper revelation of himself — the two go hand in hand. If I am ever to adequately understand myself, I must not measure myself against myself, or against people I don't like, or against my enemies, heroes, or role models. If I am ever to understand myself, I am going to need deeper insights into *who Jesus is*, for He is the standard that God has ordained.

As we look into our lives, we either believe that God has imparted within us vast potential for growth and significance that He wants to help us develop and release — or we don't. If we believe it, it is going to require cooperation from us. We will see how our own cooperation affects the development of our potential as we watch Peter's rollercoaster journey with Jesus. Hopefully, we will see a picture of our own potential for growth and significance as well.

Of course there's the flip side of the coin: We also have the potential for evil. Perhaps Charles Spurgeon said it best: "Beware of no one more than yourself. We carry our worst enemies within us."[1] But if you have called upon the Lord to deal with you in grace and mercy, take courage. The power of grace at work in your life is boundless. Believe it, live it, rejoice in it. You are finished with mediocrity.

BRAVE ENOUGH TO THINK ABOUT IT

1. *God sees the vast potential in all of us and calls us to cooperate with him in developing it.* Jesus told Simon he would be a "Rock." This was a mysterious clue to Simon's future, and Simon responded by wanting to hear more from this Jesus. God gives us clues about our potential — and we have to want to hear them. Then we are required to do what He tells us. Following him is the only path to realizing our true potential.

   a. What clues has God given you about your potential? What does He see in your future?

   b. How have you responded to Christ's perspective on your life? What more can you do?

   c. Are you working with Jesus to begin realizing your potential? What specific steps could you take to increase your partnership in his plan?

2. *Our journey with Jesus begins when we are willing to drop our own agenda and submit to his authority.* Our natural tendency is to forge our own way. But because of his compelling power in our lives, there comes a moment when we realize we need to do what He asks "because He says so." We let down our nets, even if we think that it's the *wrong* thing to do. Submitting our lives to Christ's authority, whether or not we understand it, is the key to becoming all He created us to be.

   a. When is the last time you did something you really didn't want to do, for no other reason than you were told to? What made you submit to that authority?

   b. In what areas of your life is it the most difficult to let go of your agenda? What's different about these areas that makes them tough to release?

   c. Have you put limits on what God can do with your life? What are some ways in which you might have done this?

   d. What part of your life is Christ asking you for? Are you going to give it to him?

3. *If we want to know ourselves better, first we must get to know Jesus.* When Simon Peter's boat began to sink under the load of the incredible haul of fish, he suddenly recognized Jesus as a miraculous and powerful presence in his life — capable of anything — the Messiah. Immediately upon this recognition, Peter also had a deeper revelation of *himself.* He saw his own unworthiness and powerlessness. Any delusions of self-sufficiency or righteousness were, in an instant, smashed. Seeing the true nature of Jesus is the only way we can have a true picture of ourselves — and we must have this accurate portrait of who we are before we can begin working with him to develop our potential.

   a. Have you ever had a sudden, overwhelming revelation of the true nature of God? If so, how did it change you? If not, ask God to give you that revelation.

   b. What measures have you been using to evaluate yourself? Have you been comparing yourself to others? How do you look when you compare yourself to Jesus?

   c. In what areas of your life are you committed to self-sufficiency? In what ways do you consider yourself righteous? How can you let go of these delusions?

4. *God can't begin lifting us up until we are humbled before him.* As long as we think we're the ones in control of our lives, we won't see any need to follow or obey God. But when we finally come face-to-face with our own lack of control, we realize we can't do it all on our own. This is the moment when we experience true humility, and we're ready for him to start working in us.

   a. Have you ever had a truly humbling experience? How did you react to it? Did you use it to grow, or get angry, or withdraw?

   b. What's your gut reaction to the idea of giving up control over your life? How will you ever fully be able to do this?

   c. What gives you the courage to tell Christ, "You're in charge"? What holds you back?

BRAVE ENOUH FOR ACTION

As you journey with Jesus, you might want to begin exploring your own potential. A good place to start is to make an inventory of the things that make you uniquely "you." Look at your heritage, history, and experience. Write down some of your gifts, talents, interests, aspirations, hopes, and fears. Have any opportunities or self-revelations come seemingly out of the blue? Has He given you any clues as to what He sees as your potential? Are there any signs that Jesus has been working to transform you?

chapter 2

FISHERS OF MEN

MATTHEW 4:18-22
MARK 2:1-17; 3:13-19
LUKE 5:8-11; 6:1-10

"*G*o away from me," cried Peter. *Get out of my life!*

But Jesus didn't go away.

"I'm a sinful man," Peter continued. *I'm totally unworthy.*

Jesus told him, "Don't be afraid." Then He added, "Follow me — I'll make you fish for people."

In a few brief words, Jesus offered Peter three things that He also offers each of us: a reassurance, an invitation, and a promise.

REASSURANCE

There is a certain fear of God that is totally appropriate. Solomon tells us "the fear of the LORD is the beginning of knowledge" (Proverbs 1:7). Jeremiah protested that in his day there was no fear of God (see Jeremiah 5:24), and the Greek word for "godliness" used in the New Testament has as its root idea "a sense of awe." Godly living is built upon a recognition of the awesomeness of God. There is clearly a place for godly fear.

Why, then, did Jesus tell Peter not to be afraid? There's a big difference between having a respectful sense of awe in the presence of deity and feeling terrified by an overpowering force that dominates and destroys. The second attitude sees only law and judgment and lacks an understanding of grace and mercy. Peter was right to be overwhelmed. *This Jesus is powerful — and I'm so sinful.* But he was begging to be abandoned by the One who had come to rescue him. Deep reverence was right; servile fear was wrong. As a pious Jew, Peter knew the law. He had yet to learn about grace.

So before anything else, Jesus gave him reassurance: "Don't be frightened as if I'd come to threaten you. Trust me." Jesus knew that before Peter could hear everything else He had to say, Peter needed to calm down. He needed to take comfort in Jesus' reassurance.

THE INVITATION

"Come, follow me." *Was it a command? A suggestion?* I'm sure the tone of voice Jesus used, and the look on his face, made clear that this was a firm but generous invitation. *This is the Messiah.* Peter realized Jesus was issuing a summons to join him in whatever lay ahead — in the establishing of the new era. It was a call to both fellowship and action. "Come" was an invitation to a relationship with Jesus. "Follow me" was a summons to discipleship — to be identified with him in his cause.

These two dimensions of the divine call must always be maintained in healthy balance. For to be committed to the *cause* of Christ without being in tune with the *living person* of Christ is to be linked to a purpose without being connected to the power. You can't be a *Christian* without having a *relationship* with Jesus. Yet, to be intimately related to Christ without being committed to his cause is to be attracted to a person without being attached to what He stands for. You can't say you have a relationship with Jesus, yet refuse to embrace a lifestyle aligned with his teachings. That's like an athlete who says he is committed to a coach, but doesn't intend to play for him. So "come" is a gentle invitation. "Follow me" is a serious summons to action.

Later when Jesus was teaching the people, He issued the invitation in a different way: "Come to me, all you who are weary and burdened, and I will give you rest" (Matthew 11:28). It's an invitation and a reassurance all at once. Jesus immediately added, "Take my yoke upon you and learn from me," a summons to discipleship. He added, "for I am gentle and humble in heart, and you will find rest for your souls. For my yoke is easy and my burden is light" (verses 29-30). He presented the summons along with the reassurance, because He knew we'd need the encouragement to be able to say yes. Even though his yoke is easy, it's still a yoke. His burden is light, but the call is still to be a burden bearer.

Peter already knew that following Jesus would mean being involved in establishing the long-awaited kingdom. This was exciting and promising, but it also left room for wondering and speculation. *What will I do? Where will I go? How long will it take? Will we succeed?* There were no answers to these questions, but there was one piece of information that Peter understood.

THE PROMISE

"I will make you fishers of men," Jesus said. Peter knew that fishing for fish involved catching them in a net. So it was reasonable to assume that his role would be to haul people writhing and struggling into the kingdom. Jeremiah had written, "'But now I will send for many fishermen' declares the LORD, 'and they will catch them'" (Jeremiah 16:16). Maybe that's what Jesus had come for. *Was it possible that catching men meant helping them discover the liberation of being captured by Jesus and being led by him into the adventure of a lifetime?* Maybe Peter was being asked to help other people experience what he had only just started to find himself. He didn't know, but the offer, whatever it amounted to, was being extended with quiet, compelling force.

Peter had no way of knowing what would be involved in "following" Jesus, but Jesus apparently believed Peter knew enough to make a decision. If Peter had asked for a job description of this new "fisher of men" position, he would probably have come up empty. If he had stated how many evenings he was willing to work, and how many he needed to be home to put the kids to bed, no doubt this would have stimulated some interesting discussion with the Master.

The offer was clear, yet ambiguous. It was a call to trust and commit to the One who was totally trustworthy, who had Peter's best interests at heart and would not let him down. Yet Jesus had not found it necessary to say what would be involved beyond a relationship with himself and an involvement in building the kingdom.

Peter encountered the same paradox that each of us faces when we hear Jesus calling our name. It seems to be a risky proposition —

He moves in mysterious ways, and we often don't know where He's taking us, or why. Yet there is really no risk at all, because He cannot fail. His purposes will succeed. *But it feels so out of control.*

So Peter was compelled to make a decision that would determine the course of his life. He could stay where he was, and remain for the rest of his days an unknown, unheralded fisherman in an obscure Galilean village. Or, he could launch out into the deep with Jesus and discover what happens when a man entrusts his all to God's Son. He could play it safe and stay Simon — something he knew he could handle, or he could plunge into the future with this man who seemed to know him and discover what it would mean to be Peter.

Similar choices confront every person who hears the call of Christ. Down through the years, millions have responded and found life. Yet unknown numbers have hesitated. Counting the cost and finding it too high for their liking, they have declined and settled for life without the One who Peter later discovered was "the Way, the Truth and the Life," without whom no one would ever come to the Father.

Peter looked around him. The lake shimmering in the heat of the day, the haze settling over the mountains. The occasional fish leaping for an unsuspecting fly, the birds swooping low over the water. His boats and neatly piled nets, and a little bit off the beach his small fisherman's cottage. His young wife sitting in the shade of a vine, talking quietly with her mother. His friends James and John, his brother Andrew, the men he had known from childhood.

Everything that made his life the solid, unspectacular existence he had known from youth was there. The pleasant life of a simple fisherman — it was all he'd ever wanted, all he'd thought he ever needed. It was all there and Jesus was asking him to leave it and strike out for — what? *He wants me to trade the familiar for the unfamiliar, the known for the unknown, the predictable for the unpredictable. Should I or shouldn't I?*

Jesus stood by quietly as Peter wrestled in his soul. He gave Peter a reassuring smile, but said nothing. There was nothing else to say. It was decision time.

"I'll do it," Peter blurted out. "I'll come with you."

"I knew you would," Jesus replied. "James, John, and Andrew are coming, too," He added. "We'll leave in the morning." And with that He walked away to the hills, as He so often did.

This extraordinary, life-changing moment in Peter's life was brought to mind a number of years ago when my wife and I were aboard a ship in the Baltic Sea. The water was extremely turbulent, and the small pilot boat that had come alongside to take the pilot home was experiencing great difficulty. The pilot had brought his young son, and the boy was clearly terrified as he contemplated jumping from the heaving deck of the larger boat to the slippery tossing deck of the smaller vessel. The father jumped first, landing safely without difficulty, but the boy froze. It seemed like an age before the boy, hearing his father shout, "jump now" in a commanding tone, did so and found himself warmly embraced in loving arms. There was a beautiful blend of command in the father's voice and comfort in his embrace, which the boy only discovered when he jumped. So it is with the call of Christ.

He does not fill in the blanks. He does not discuss the fine points. He doesn't have to. He chooses not to answer all the questions, and at times appears to ignore some of the fears. All He does is show us who He is, prove He is totally reliable, and give us the opportunity to jump and discover that He cares for us in love and envisions for us a future beyond imagination.

The call of Jesus was, and still is, short on detail but full of promise. Jesus offered Peter the chance to be actively involved in preparations for the coming kingdom, and He offers the same prospect to each of us. For Peter, and for us, to respond is to accept an invitation to significance. It is an incredible opportunity to know God in an intimate and personal way, and deepen that relationship so that each of us would begin to have an impact in the world.

So with his acceptance of the invitation, Peter's journey with Jesus began. It was nonstop excitement. Peter stood by as Jesus healed everyone from lepers to paralytics and spent days on end teaching the growing multitude, inspiring awe and controversy wherever He went. The constant pressure of the crowds took its toll, and Jesus escaped whenever possible into the hillside. He loved the quiet. It gave him a chance to pray.

One evening Jesus slipped away quietly, but when He had not returned early the next morning, Peter went looking for him in the dark. "Everyone is searching for you," Peter explained. Like any good fisherman, Peter knew that when the fish are running, you drop whatever you're doing, grab your nets, strike out from shore, and seize the moment. The people were looking for Jesus, so this was no time for him to be sitting quietly in a solitary place. Action-oriented guys like Peter seldom understand those of a more contemplative nature. People who prefer solitude shake their heads at people who are always on the go. Jesus, of course, belonged in neither extreme. He understood that in quietness and communion with the Father, the resources for action are found.

Jesus told Peter, "Alright. Let's go. We've a lot of work to do." And they set out for the villages dotted around the lake and on the hillside (Mark 1:35-39).

Local people mobbed Jesus wherever He went, but on one occasion things got a little out of hand. A group of men were bringing their friend to Jesus, but they could not get close to him because of the crowd. Scripture doesn't specify, but some scholars think this took place at Peter's house. The men climbed onto the roof and started to dismantle it while Jesus was talking to the people below. When the hole was big enough, they lowered their friend on a mat right down in front of Jesus. This great demonstration of faith on the part of the men who dug the hole in the roof, and an even greater faith on the part of the man on the mat, caught everybody's attention. Jesus didn't comment on the man's physical problems but said, "Son, your sins are forgiven." He recognizes that regardless of our physical problems, we all have more crucial underlying spiritual issues for which we need the gracious touch of God. This Jesus graciously provided to the paralytic.

But there were some Pharisees there who were not prepared to be so gracious. They were horrified when Jesus said the man's sins were forgiven. "Who can forgive sins but God alone?" they asked themselves. They were right, of course, but they did not recognize that Jesus was God incarnate. Jesus read their minds. "What's easier?" He asked. "To forgive sins or to heal bodies?" Then, to show that neither posed a problem for him, He told the man to get up, pick up his mat, and walk home. The man did, and the people marveled — except the Pharisees. They were livid.

Later Jesus continued alongside the sea, teaching the crowds. Peter and his friends followed along, eager to hear what Jesus would say and perhaps even more eager to see what He would do. They did not have to wait long. In a booth on the main highway sat Levi — the most unpopular man in town. He worked for the Romans, and his job was collecting taxes. These taxes were deeply resented and the tax collectors were utterly despised. Levi was a parasite in the minds of the local people — a traitor. So you can imagine the looks of scorn, the sly remarks, and the outright belligerence the crowds sent his way as they walked past his booth.

But Jesus went over to talk to him. They were deep in conversation. Then to the utter astonishment of the crowd, they heard him say to Levi, "Follow me." The familiar call. He was asking this wretched man to join them. Unbelievably, Levi jumped up, shut up his booth, and joined the crowd. Peter must have been incredulous. *A tax collector gets the same invitation? The identical summons extended to James, John, and me?*

Some time later, Levi invited Jesus and some of his men to dinner at his home. The Pharisees, who by this time were following Jesus everywhere, asked the disciples, "Why does he eat with tax collectors and sinners?" Peter and the disciples looked at each other, hesitating to answer. *That's a good question.* So Jesus answered, telling his inquisitors that healthy people don't need doctors, but sick people do. They got the point. He had come looking for people whose lives were messed up in order to get them back on track. He was not looking for people who were on track and needed no help, or who thought they didn't need help because they imagined they were okay. The Pharisees didn't like his answer—or his attitude. Peter sensed trouble was brewing, for these Pharisees were not people to be taken lightly.

The Pharisees were to be commended for their desire to live according to the Law. But their attempts to get it right had backfired on them as they struggled to fill in the details that were not spelled out in the Book of the Law. For instance, the Law said the people should honor the Lord by not working on the Sabbath. The Pharisees considered manual labor to be one example of "work." So they went around keeping an eye open for anyone who might be doing anything close to manual labor, such as carrying a load or lighting a fire.

Soon after the calling of Levi, Peter and his friends were walking with Jesus through a grain field on a Sabbath morning. They casually picked a few grains and ate them. This was not a problem for Jesus. But the Pharisees, always watching, loudly proclaimed, "Look, they are doing what is unlawful on the Sabbath!" To their way of thinking, the act of plucking a few grains amounted to manual labor and therefore contravened Sabbath law. Jesus had little patience with this kind of legalistic nit-picking and He let the Pharisees know it. When shortly afterward on the Sabbath He confronted a man who needed healing, He intentionally healed him and dared the Pharisees to say that it was wrong to do good on the Sabbath. He made it abundantly clear that He would not tolerate such hard-hearted, legalistic attitudes.

Tensions were rising. It was only a matter of time before there would be a showdown with these powerful men. They were threatened by the popularity of Jesus and were scandalized by the way He was challenging their long-cherished systems of belief. Peter and his friends were caught up in something that was way beyond anything they had imagined. Never had they seen such adulation as the crowds heaped on Jesus. They had not witnessed such spiritual hunger in the people, and they had never seen such remarkable miracles. Certainly, they had not anticipated the antagonism and bitter hatred from these religious men who watched their every move and waited like lions to pounce on any false step.

Eventually, Jesus stayed out of the towns as much as possible, and the people came to him in the remote areas. The crowds had become unmanageable, and it became evident that Jesus needed to share the load. One day He withdrew and went up onto a hillside. He sent word for a dozen handpicked men from the huge crowd of disciples. He invited them personally to come to him. It says in Mark 3, He "called to him those he wanted."

No doubt He could have picked more than twelve, but there are reasons to believe He chose this number because of the significance of the twelve tribes of Israel and the fact that eventually those twelve would be given twelve thrones from which they would oversee the judgment of the twelve tribes. But this was hidden from the men as they trudged up the mountainside wondering why Jesus had called them there.

He told them that He had specifically chosen them to fulfill a very significant role. Their first priority would be to spend time with him, both for his benefit and theirs. He needed their support and friendship. They needed the special training they would receive as they lived in close proximity to him. Then He told them his plan to share with them the load of preaching to the great crowds demanding his attention. They were to watch how He spoke, to listen attentively to his message, and to develop their skills in communicating the good news that they were now learning from him. In addition, they would need to address the prevailing problem they were confronting on a daily basis — the problem of demonic activity. Jesus proposed sharing with them his authority over the demons that seemed to inhabit so many people.

We have no record of the response of these untrained men to this high calling, but it is not difficult to imagine their mixed emotions as they realized they were about to be thrust out to the front line of what was becoming a more challenging and perilous enterprise. There would be satisfaction at the thought of being specially chosen by Jesus and a sense of privilege in being invested with authority over the dark powers with which they were so familiar and yet they inadequately understood. But they had seen enough of the demands of ministry and the tensions from opposing forces to know that they were not being called to a picnic. *We're being mobilized for battle.* A battle for the souls of men and women that was not to be taken lightly.

"I'm going to call you apostles," Jesus explained to the men sitting on the hillside. Little did these men realize that this private, unheralded moment would change the face of the whole world. These men were being commissioned to go far beyond their beloved Galilee to represent Jesus, to proclaim his message, to further his cause, to perpetuate his memory, and to be the foundation stones of his worldwide church. Never in the history of the human race had such a simple event carried such a weight of world-changing possibilities. Thousands of years later some of these humble men would be household names around the world. Cathedrals would bear their names, cities would be named after them, countries would make them their patron saints, their flags would fly over the centers of power in scores of lands, proud parents down through the centuries in a hundred languages would give their newborn sons the names of these Galilean men. And nobody would have been more astonished to hear this than the twelve Jesus chose.

Over the years various lists of these twelve men have appeared in sacred writings. The order was never the same but there was one peculiarity. Every list started with the same name: *Simon, to whom Jesus gave the name Peter.* This man was a leader in the making, a rough diamond about to be polished, a work in progress. He was an ordinary man whose hidden potential was to be unearthed and put on display to the glory of God and the untold blessing of mankind. But none of this would happen overnight.

BRAVE ENOUGH TO THINK ABOUT IT

1. *In the face of our own sinfulness, we don't need to be afraid of God.* Sometimes our unworthiness compels us to hide from God, even tell him to go away. But Christ tells us, "Don't be afraid." He means it. Fear paralyzes and renders us unable to take the next step — believing his promise, accepting his invitation, and following him.

   a. What other words besides "afraid" would describe your reaction to God's display of power in your life? Do you believe him when He says there's no need to fear him?

   b. Do you ever hide from God or act as if He's not there? What specific events or experiences have triggered your acting this way? Are you still doing it?

   c. When have you felt unworthy in the presence of God? How did you respond? What would be the appropriate response?

2. *Christ invites us to follow him, and He expects a response.* We often hear people saying, "I accepted Christ at the age of . . ." But what's really amazing is not that we accept Christ, but that He accepts us. He invites us personally to come to him. The Scripture says He "called to him those he wanted, and they came." They said, "yes, I'll be there." God in Christ is still inviting people, still calling people, still offering people the opportunity to discover their divinely imparted significance and to release their unknown potential.

   a. Have you heard the invitation from Christ? If so, when was it? What did it look or sound like?

   b. Have you responded? What was your response? How has your life changed since then?

   c. What does it mean to you that He invited you? Have you taken it for granted? Have you considered what a privilege it is?

3. *Following Jesus involves risk, uncertainty, and stepping out into the unknown.* When we commit our lives to him, we've no idea where He's going to take us. Our lives could totally change and there's the possibility that

we'll face unimaginable challenges. But our assurance comes from knowing God is in control, and in his hands, we cannot fail. Making the decision to step out despite the risk can be a transforming moment in our lives.

a. What sorts of risky things do you enjoy doing? What makes them appeal to you? What risks do you *not* enjoy? Why not?

b. In what ways does following Christ seem risky? Does the risk seem appealing or objectionable?

c. Have you experienced challenges in your life that you may not have had if you weren't a believer? If so, was it worth it?

4. *Christ's call on our lives gives us a deeper understanding of our own purpose.* Jesus promised Peter, "From now on you will catch men." Peter realized Jesus had something in mind for him, however vague it appeared at the moment. Peter left what he was doing and followed Jesus. He committed. Understanding that we have a *purpose* in Christ leads to a sense of *commitment* to the One who will enable us to fulfill the potential He has placed in us.

a. What is your current understanding — whether clear or vague — of what Christ is calling you to do? What is your God-given purpose?

b. What are some strategies you could use to conquer any reluctance you may have about making a commitment to Christ?

c. Do you find it easier to trust your eternal destiny to Christ than to trust him with your immediate future? If so, why?

BRAVE ENOUGH FOR ACTION

Every time the gospel is proclaimed, everybody within the sound of that gospel receives an invitation to significance. Have you RSVPed? Have you become a disciple of Jesus Christ? If so, take a moment to write down what it means to you to be a disciple. If not, consider taking that step. Either way, write down or discuss what your next step might be. How can you take your spiritual experience to another level? Is there any part of you that rejects this idea? Why?

chapter 3

HILLSIDE CLASSROOM

MATTHEW 5:1—7:29; 9:35—10:42

*P*eter and the other eleven men had been introduced to elementary discipleship. They understood that Jesus was unique and that the crowds responded to him. He had challenged them, and they had responded. They had become aware that Jesus' mission would provoke formidable challenges from powerful people. Nevertheless, although they were short on details, these daring men had packed their bags, left their homes, and cast their lot with Jesus. They were ready and eager to learn, to follow, and to advance his cause. So far, so good.

Peter's knowledge of Jesus, while it was growing all the time, was still severely limited. His understanding of what Jesus meant by "the kingdom" was woefully deficient. But this was to be expected. Jesus had only begun teaching; He would continue, and Peter was willing to learn.

This next step in Peter's journey with Jesus would be an intense tutorial on a different and sometimes difficult approach to life. Peter listened as Jesus gave sermon after sermon, sometimes clarifying familiar points of Jewish law, but in most cases, turning it upside down and inside out. Everything Peter knew about life and the Law was subject to new interpretation. He certainly had his "Aha!" moments when something Jesus said suddenly made sense; he had more moments of frustration and bewilderment. *What in the world is Jesus talking about?* At this point, all Jesus asked of Peter was for him to listen attentively and do his best to take it all in. What exactly were these surprising teachings?

One of the first lessons that may have raised an eyebrow was when Jesus said, "You are the salt of the earth." Peter knew salt was an effective preservative because he packed his catch in it before sending it to market. *I'm going to be a preservative?* What would he preserve? Salt also improves the flavor of food. Peter might have surmised that he was to bring the "flavor" of the good news to the people, sprinkling it out on them like salt, in some way saving or preserving them. The Master underlined this when He added, "You are the light of the world." The disciples were to let their light "shine before men," that is, they could not keep all these new teachings to themselves. Their lives would give light and direction to men and women, and God would be praised for the way they lived.

These were challenging concepts. The men were being told that Jesus expects practical, everyday transformation in the lives of his people. There would be no more of the dry, powerless religion that argues about niceties and ignores tragedies. He wanted them to be thinking "salt" and "light" all the time. There's enough darkness around that needs banishing. There's no shortage of corruption that cries out for a cleanup.

So Peter and the disciples would play a major role in preaching the message of the kingdom. Jesus taught that life in this kingdom was a "blessed" life. *Makes sense*, Peter thought. But then it became apparent that Jesus' ideas of blessedness and his were miles apart. His Jewish heritage had taught him that the blessed man is one who doesn't walk in the ways of the ungodly or stand in the way of sinners. Rather, the blessed man spends time studying and applying the law of the Lord. Peter had done this. But then Jesus said that the blessed life of the kingdom would be enjoyed by "the poor in spirit," "those who mourn," "the meek," those who were "hungry and thirsty for righteousness," the "pure in heart," the "peacemakers," and the "persecuted." *Pure and righteous, yes — but meek? Persecuted? Mourning?* It didn't seem right. Peter had a lot of learning to do. (Most times, I feel the same way.)

Peter and the other disciples were not going to understand these new teachings until they first unlearned some things that were deeply ingrained. The Rabbis had taught them they could live by the "letter" of the law, but ignore the spirit. Jesus took aim at this kind of hypocrisy and elevated their understanding of moral and godly living to new heights. From his teaching, they learned that adultery started in the heart, not in the bed; that murder can be committed by the weapon of anger; and that common attitudes about divorce were unacceptable because they victimized women and degraded marriage.

They were amazed when He told them to love their enemies rather than operate under the well known "eye for an eye" rule, and that if attacked they should invite another blow before considering hitting back. *What, are you kidding?* This would have been a foreign concept to a rugged Galilean fisherman. Jesus told them to be willing to forgive if they expected forgiveness. He pointed out the inconsistency of worshiping money while professing to worship the Lord. He told them that there was no point to worrying about life's little details, because the Father in heaven knew what they needed and was perfectly capable of supplying their needs. Jesus also told them to practice their spiritual disciplines quietly and privately, in contrast to the common practice of some who made an impressive public show of giving alms, fasting, and praying so that people would mark their piety. On and on it went, one firmly held notion after another dropping like flies.

Jesus went on to challenge them about their tendency to be judgmental, expose their blatant hypocrisies, and warn them of the dangers of empty professions of faith that were not backed by lives of trusting obedience. He summarized his powerful teaching by saying that hearing what He told them was not enough — they had to do what He said. In fact, if they heard what He said and did not do it, they would be as stupid as a man who builds his house on sand — in other words, they would be inviting disaster. Obedience to his words would lead to a secure, solid life, like a house built on a solid foundation.

It was becoming apparent to Peter that this was a refreshingly different approach to life. Jesus was speaking out against legalism, insisting on a life of obedience springing from a heart of love for the

Lord. He was presenting a spiritual experience that touched every dimension of life. *This is not just about religion. It's about money, and work, and relationships . . . it's about life.*

Peter and the other disciples had always thought that the "kingdom" would be a powerful political entity — that when the Messiah came, He would take his place in government and reign over them as King. Jesus was saying — but they were not yet hearing — that, on the contrary, the kingdom He had come to establish was not a political entity, but a spiritual reality. It was all about the rule of God in the hearts of men and women. It would be carried in their hearts by an understanding of God's love for sinners, and would spill over into love for God, which would lead to trusting obedience and faith. It would lead to authentic caring for others. But they had a long way to go before they grasped the message.

Even though Jesus dealt in lofty subjects, He framed them in captivating yet everyday stories. He touched on the great themes of human existence by telling simple tales about daily life. The crowds couldn't get enough of his parables. Not that they always understood them — in fact, even the twelve apostles missed the point at times. Occasionally they requested and received special interpretations.

Jesus was well aware that there were many in the crowd who were following him and listening to his stories for no other reason than because He was "the best show in town." On the other hand, there were also people who were hungry for righteousness and reality. So Jesus' parables served to amuse and inform the peripheral people, while stimulating the earnest seekers to dig beneath the surface. I often notice this same pattern in churches today. How many of us are there on Sunday morning because it's just "the thing to do"? We get lively music and preaching that's funny, topical, and not too in-your-face — an amusing way to spend an hour. Yet, many others are sincerely seeking truth and life. Jesus, the ultimate teacher, knew how to speak to both types of people, and was particularly adept in teaching with parables.

For instance, in one of his most famous stories, Jesus demon-strated the different attitudes of his listeners. As He was walking and preaching, He may have passed a farmer with a basket of seed under his arm, scattering seed across his roughly plowed field. The farmer sowed liberally and indiscriminately, so some of the seed fell on rocky ground, some among thorns and thistles, some on a hard path, and only a part of the seed fell on good ground where it had a chance to grow and eventually be fruitful. Jesus told his followers that his teachings were like the seed, and their reactions were like the soil. Only a few people — the ones who heard the words of Jesus and understood — were like the seed that fell on good soil and pro-duced good fruit. Everyone else was unfavorable soil, failing to allow his words to sink in and develop, so they produced no fruit. Peter wondered, *What kind of soil am I?*

In a similar vein, Jesus talked about fishermen catching a mixed bag of fish in their nets. Some they could use, others they threw away. Some of his listeners would make an honest response to his words; others would appear to do so but would not be genuine. Jesus said that likewise, at the end of the age, wicked people would be separated from the righteous. The more Peter listened, the more he began to realize the challenge that Jesus was presenting to him. *Good fish or bad fish? Good soil or bad soil?* This was powerful teaching presented in disarmingly simple fashion.

THE LORD'S PRAYER

There was plenty of food for thought as the days of learning continued. But something began to bother the twelve men. When Jesus excused himself and retreated to a remote place to pray, He did it quietly and for extended periods. Sometimes He was gone all night. By comparison, their prayer lives left much to be desired. They were caught up in centuries-old praying traditions, most often speaking rote words rather than petitioning or praising God from their hearts. So, one of the group asked Jesus if He would teach them to pray. He gladly responded and passed on to them what we now call the Lord's Prayer.

Some people see this as a prayer that should be memorized and repeated word for word. Others see it as a model prayer that outlines the kind of things that God's people should incorporate into their praying. Either way, an informal study of the prayer reveals depths of insight that can bring great blessing as we learn to pray based on this model.

First, Jesus taught that we can pray to God as Father. Fathers know what their children need, and enjoy meeting their needs. This might seem obvious to us today, but in Peter's day, God was seen as much more remote than a close family member. Praying to God as

Father immediately helps us to see the importance of our personal relationship with him. But in case our intimacy should become casual and careless, Jesus pointed out that God is the Father *in heaven*, great, grand, and glorious. He advised us to start our prayers focused on the concerns of the Father, rather than our own worries. We should honor God's name and his person. We should express a desire to see God's kingdom actually come into being. We should long to see God's will become paramount in the interests of men and women.

Once these priorities are firmly in place, it's appropriate for us to pray about more personal and mundane matters, such as "daily bread." We can and should talk to the Lord about the necessities of life, avoiding taking for granted the provision of daily needs. Next, we should talk to the Lord about our struggles with relationships, especially forgiving and accepting forgiveness. Jesus also recognized that we would all be subjected to temptations that would be difficult to overcome. He said that we should bring our feelings of weakness and vulnerability to the Lord in prayer, seeking his enabling to deal with the issues that could lead to spiritual disaster and downfall.

Jesus taught his disciples that they should pray about all these things, and in so doing, they would not only find their relationship with the heavenly Father deepened and enriched, but they would find practical answers to the challenges of life. As Peter took it all in, there was one thing he could not overlook. It was clear that Jesus felt that He needed to pray — and if Jesus did, of course, Peter knew he needed to all the more.

The teaching on prayer was followed by many more lessons — fasting, money, worry, charity, enemies, criticizing others — no subject was left uncovered. We don't know how much of this instruction the disciples received at any one time, and we can assume it was difficult to assimilate so much new information at once. Certain clues a little later in the journey tell us that Peter and the other men weren't necessarily taking it all in quite yet. But that's not surprising considering that they'd just begun their "classroom" learning. Everything was just words at this point. Like all good education programs, the next step would be some on-the-job-training — the disciples' internship.

STEPPING OUT

Jesus' ministry was rapidly developing on two fronts. Huge crowds of people were demanding — and receiving — his attention. But at the same time He was concentrating on training the twelve apostles. So He was busy dealing with the crowds on one level and training the Twelve on another.

Jesus decided it was time for their training to take a quantum leap. Looking at the crowds, He commented that they looked to him like harassed and helpless sheep who had lost their shepherd. This was not said critically, but compassionately. Isaiah the prophet had noted that human beings are like sheep that have gone astray (see Isaiah 53:6). Like sheep, we have a tendency to wander away from the safety of the fold, putting ourselves in harm's way. Jesus had often seen lost, wandering, torn, and bedraggled sheep bleating out their misery, and the people in the crowds looked similar. He was the good Shepherd, He loved the sheep, He had come to seek and save them, and He had every intention of laying down his life for the sheep at the appropriate moment. But first the people had to be warned about the coming kingdom that would be like a great sheepfold, and they could be welcomed into the fold. They needed to learn that the entrance to this fold was through repentance.

The Twelve heard Jesus describe the people, saw the pain in his eyes, and realized that He had a depth of compassion they couldn't fathom. He told them that there was a vast harvest of people waiting to be reached for the kingdom, but there was a chronic shortage of workers and they should start praying that the Father would thrust more workers out to do the work of announcing the kingdom and calling people to repentance. Peter wondered how the Father was going to provide more workers. He soon found out. *I'm going to be part of the answer to my own prayers.*

Jesus had already promised to make them fishers of men. Now they were going to become workers in the harvest and shepherds of lost sheep. Whatever picture Jesus used, Peter began to realize that he was about to hit the road.

Jesus called the Twelve together and explained to them how necessary it was for the people of Israel to be alerted to the fact that the kingdom was about to dawn upon them. Someone had to tell them, and only those who knew about it could do it. These twelve men knew the message, even if they still did not comprehend it.

He calmly instructed them about their assignment. They were to travel among the people of Israel. They were to be very specific in their message: They were to teach what they had heard from John the Baptist and repeat what they had heard from Jesus. They had been listening to his teaching for quite awhile now. This was their chance to pass on what they had discovered.

Peter stood by, silent. He looked hard at Jesus as doubts flooded his mind. *How will I get the crowds to listen to me? I can't perform miracles, cure diseases, or exorcise demons. I'm not Jesus. I'm not ready.* He looked around him — Andrew, James, John, and the other men were similarly at a loss. None of them was any more promising, or any more confident.

But Jesus did not seem at all anxious. These were his men and He was in charge. He knew their understanding of the kingdom was inadequate at best, and dead wrong at worst, but He was going to send them anyway. If these men were ever to become proficient in the ministry to which He had called them, they would have to start somewhere. He would have to allow them time to make mistakes and give them a chance to learn by doing. There are some things that cannot be learned in the classroom — even if the classroom is the wide open spaces of the hills overlooking Galilee and the distinguished professor is Jesus himself. Reassuringly, Jesus told them that He was giving them the power and authority to exorcise demons and heal people's infirmities.

They weren't being called to teach foreign subjects. They were being commissioned to articulate what they had been given every chance to know. Jesus never expects his people to say what they don't know. Neither does He grant them the freedom of keeping quiet about what they have learned. The rule of thumb for Jesus' disciples is: *we're not expected to speak authoritatively about matters of which we are ignorant, and we're not expected to stay silent on issues about which we have been enlightened.* Plus, He gives us the power and authority we'll need to speak up.

So Peter and the other men headed out. No suitcases, no coolers of food and drinks, no hotel reservations. Talk about a road trip — this was flying by the seat of their pants. Peter wondered about the details. *Where will we stay? How will we eat?* The answer Jesus gave can be summarized briefly as "don't worry about it." Jesus was confident that the Father would not leave his men out on a limb and that in every village there would be at least one decent person who would extend basic hospitality to strangers. But in the unlikely event that help was not forthcoming, they should simply leave town and go somewhere else. They would not be greeted with open arms everywhere they went. There would be hostile responses to them and their message, so they should keep their eyes open and watch their backs! If and when things got a little rough, they should not be unduly worried because the worst that men could do to them was kill their bodies — no man could touch their souls. Their focus should be on pleasing the Lord, rather than being afraid of people.

The worst that could happen is . . . I could be killed? Peter was finally getting an accurate picture of this discipleship gig. Jesus was not trying to scare them, but alert them to the realities of reaching the world with a message that's not always the one people want to hear. Jesus didn't paint any glowing pictures. He refused to send the men out on a wave of unrealistic euphoria, preferring to outline the very real difficulties they would face.

Sometimes the harsh realities of a project are kept hidden from those being recruited because if the truth were known, nobody would sign up. People can only handle so much reality. This approach can lead to promising recruitment and devastating fallout. Jesus knew it was far better to work with a dedicated few who are committed despite the hardships, rather than a larger group intent on getting out of what they unwittingly got into. Jesus never sugarcoated the truth in order to get people to participate in anything. On this occasion, He actually said they were being sent out like sheep in the midst of wolves. His men were not deterred, and like sheep they headed out to where they knew the wolves were waiting.

They were on a steep learning curve. They had no doubts about the authority that Jesus wielded. He was able to draw on heaven's authority, and they had yet to see anything powerful enough to resist him. Still, it's one thing to believe what Jesus says in a classroom or a pew — the place where so often the life of faith begins. But for faith to flourish it must step out — if not among wolves, at least out of our comfort zone. So Peter had to go to the people, stand tall in their presence, and proclaim loudly and clearly, *"In the name of Jesus . . ."* In doing this, he was not only stating his association with Jesus, he was also making it clear that any ability on his part to achieve anything wonderful came from Jesus and not from Peter.

Amazingly, it worked. In the cities and towns, people were freed from their bondage to demons at the command of the disciples. They spoke, and sufferers were healed. The miracles were the attention grabbers, capturing the people's interest. Then the apostles followed up with the proclamation of the kingdom. Their actions established credibility, then they used their credibility to communicate the message. It was an exciting internship, filled with successes and the heady exhilaration of accomplishing things previously unimagined.

Jesus had arranged for his disciples to put into practice what they had heard and seen in his classroom. They had been commissioned to learn by doing. This is how quantum growth takes place in the life of the disciple. Provided, of course, that the disciple will take the plunge.

Our brash disciple Peter was certainly willing to step out. But many of us are not so eager, and therein lies the biggest problem for those of us who would be disciples: reluctance to try.

The fear of failure is one of the most debilitating factors known to mankind. We've all been conditioned by wisdom such as, "If it's worth doing, it's worth doing well." We have a deep dislike for mediocrity. We abhor halfhearted, second-best efforts. But Jesus knew the difference between inferior and simply not-yet-polished. He had drafted average men, sent them to represent him in less-than-perfect ministries, and blessed their efforts. Why? He knew they would only develop by starting badly and getting better. He knew that, in the end, it's not the perfection of the instrument, but the skill of the artist that produces the finest music. Peter allowed himself to be the instrument upon which Jesus performed. And that is all He asks of each of us.

BRAVE ENOUGH TO THINK ABOUT IT

1. *We must continually study the Word, even when we don't understand it, trusting that He gives us understanding as we need it.* Peter and the disciples heard the Word straight from the Master, but they didn't always get the message, and the result was a painfully slow process of change taking place in their lives. Still they persevered, continuing to follow Jesus and hear his teachings, even when they were completely perplexed by what they heard.

   a. What's your response to the Word when you don't get it? Do you keep studying in hopes of getting to a comfortable understanding? Do you ignore it or reject it?

   b. How are you persevering in your study of God's Word? What, exactly, does this look like in your life?

   c. What evidence is there that your understanding is growing?

2. *Christ's truth is different from the world's "truth."* Christianity involves numerous ideas that are unpopular, contrary to accepted thought, or seemingly illogical. Jesus challenged the disciples with his teachings, turning many of their firmly held notions upside down. When we study Scripture, we're likewise asked to reconsider things we thought were true.

   a. What are some specific teachings in Scripture that have challenged you personally? What ideas does our culture or education system teach that Jesus contradicts?

   b. How do you respond to scriptural ideas that you don't agree with? Do you have a tendency to reject them outright? Are there any ideas you've changed your mind about? What are they?

   c. How do you respond to the following ideas?

      · You are supposed to be salt and light to the world.

      · Blessed are the meek, the poor in spirit, and the persecuted.

      · Don't fight back, but turn the other cheek.

·Your anger is the same as committing murder, and your lustful thoughts are the same as committing adultery.

3. *Even as new believers, we're called to step into ministry and help bring others to the kingdom.* Long before the disciples would have felt they were ready, Jesus sent them out to travel all over Israel, healing sickness, casting out demons, and proclaiming the message of Christ. They were fresh converts, and Jesus used their enthusiasm to help spread the good news. He knew that the best way to get started is just to take the first step, and He pressed them to "just do it."

   a. In your experience, what's the best way to discover and develop a skill — by reading and talking about it or by jumping in and giving it a try? What examples can you think of in your own life?

   b. Why are you sometimes reluctant to put into practice what you're still learning? What are some ways to get past this?

   c. How is Christ calling you to step into ministry, either for the first time or just a step further? What is He asking you to do? What can you do immediately to get started? Are you going to do it?

4. *Jesus knows we're reluctant to step out like sheep among wolves, and He gives us all the resources we'll need to accomplish his work.* The disciples knew they were inadequate for the job, but Jesus reassured them that He had given them the power they needed. This may have been their first experience in depending on him, instead of their own skills and intelligence, to get a job done.

   a. How does the idea of "dependence on Christ" strike you? What's your general view of dependence versus independence?

   b. Do you really believe that Jesus will empower you to do the things He calls you to? Or is your belief tempered by "real world" considerations? What are they?

   c. In what ways have you already been empowered by Christ to do things you couldn't have done previously? What specific resources do you need him to give you for the next step in your journey?

BRAVE ENOUGH FOR ACTION

Whether we've been faithfully following Jesus for decades or we're brand-new believers, we can be sure He wants us to step out and be salt and light to the world. Think about where you are in your discipleship and ask yourself, *What's next? Besides continuing to study and learn, what can I do to start bringing others into the kingdom?* Pray and ask the Father the same questions. Is there one thing, one tiny step you can take immediately, to show Jesus that you're willing to brave the wolves?

chapter 4

MEAGER RESOURCES, DIVINE PROVISION

MATTHEW 14:13-36
MARK 6:30-56
JOHN 6

$\mathcal{P}$eter and the other disciples returned from their first mission trip exhausted but excited. The enormous pressures of ministry and the emotional intensity of the experience were such that Jesus decided the Twelve needed a break. There were also some troubling signs in the attitudes of the disciples. They talked incessantly about demons succumbing to their orders and people being healed. Nothing wrong with that, but they seemed to be excited about it happening through them. They were in danger of being eager for ministry because of the way it reflected positively on themselves, rather than being thrilled that people were being blessed and God was being glorified. It's a trap. Jesus knew it and He decided the men needed a break. Reflection time.

Jesus also needed time for personal quiet and reflection. He had just received word that Herod had executed John the Baptist, his forerunner, the fearless preacher of righteousness. This was an immense loss to Jesus, and He needed time to grieve the passing of this great man. So for two big reasons, Jesus and the Twelve set out across the lake for a time of renewal and refreshment.

But their time of quiet was not to be. Word had gotten out that they were heading to the eastern shore, and the people were in hot pursuit of them. By the time Jesus and his men arrived, a huge crowd had gathered to greet them. Peter saw a problem. *Can't we dodge them? We need a break.* But Jesus recognized an opportunity. He looked into the faces of the people and saw great need that demanded his attention. So putting aside his own needs, He set to work ministering to the people.

Jesus seemed to derive strength from ministering, and He appeared to be stimulated by meeting needs. Far from seeking to escape, He immersed himself in people's lives and, as He did, He gave every impression of drawing energy from an invisible but seemingly infinite source. *What's the secret?* Peter wondered. *I'm so tired. Why isn't He?* It began to dawn on Peter and the disciples that the strength that comes directly from the Father is not abstract or metaphorical, but real. They realized that Jesus was drawing his fortitude directly from the Father by trusting him to provide. In their own weakness, they could be strong. Even when tired, they discovered they didn't have to be weary of doing good.

These disciples were nothing if not practical. They knew they could not match Jesus in the spiritual dimension. But they did think they could help him in the down-to-earth aspects of life. He had become so absorbed in ministering to the people, He had overlooked the fact that it was getting late. He was meeting needs; they were watching the clock. The crowds of people were far from home, they had no food or shelter, and it was time Jesus dismissed them and sent them on their way. The disciples suggested this to Jesus and were stunned when He calmly told them, "No, they're staying. You feed them." Peter looked at the crowd. *They're not our problem.* Jesus disagreed. "Oh, yes they are."

We don't know Peter's reaction, but Andrew and Philip took the instruction seriously. Philip did some rapid calculation and worked out that if they spent all the money they had at the going rate for fresh bread, they might be able to give everybody a little. That was assuming that bread was available, which it wasn't. So much for a reasonable, calculated response.

Andrew, meanwhile, had gone on a scouting expedition to see what kind of food the people had in their possession. All he had to show for his trouble was one young boy who had packed a dinner of a few little loaves and a couple of fish. He marched this boy up to Jesus, announced that he had five loaves and two fishes, and then said despairingly, "But what are they among so many?" *Right.* Peter looked on, doubtfully. *There are five thousand families here.*

Jesus took the food — we're not told what the boy thought about this appropriation of his meal — and He gave thanks. He did not bless the food — He blessed the Father. Then He gave it to the disciples and told them to get busy distributing dinner. To the amazement of the Twelve who were co-opted into this apparently futile exercise, the food began multiplying as they kept on serving, and the people kept on eating. In fact the people didn't just eat — they overate. Jesus commented later that they had gorged themselves like animals — stuffed themselves like pigs. They were not very tidy, so Jesus instructed that the leftover food be gathered up. One of the disciples with an eye for detail noted that they'd collected twelve baskets full. One for each disciple to carry down the hill?

The crowds were understandably thrilled with this provision, not only because it was abundant, but because it was free. Here was a man who could do for them what they wanted. He could meet their needs painlessly, promptly, and cheaply. And not even mention taxes. This was the kind of man they would like in a position of political power. He should be king. The idea spread throughout the crowd like a wildfire — first a murmur, and then a rising crescendo, until they were on their feet shouting, "Jesus for king. Jesus for king."

Now the disciples may have been open to this idea, given the way they were struggling with the concept of the kingdom Jesus was announcing. They were not entirely devoid of personal ambition, and they were smart enough to see that if Jesus became king, they would not be far from the seat of power and influence.

Jesus recognized what was going on and determined to put a stop to it. He ushered his disciples down the hill to the lakeside and told them to get in the boat and cross over to the other side. In fact He "made" or "constrained" them to get into the boat. Surely an odd thing for him to do, given that the men were ready to go home and boats were their normal means of transport. Why force them? Presumably because they did not want to get in the boat. But why?

We can only guess, but it may be that they were so enamored with the idea of Jesus being king that they did not want to miss the moment. There was a mass movement underway and they wanted to be part of it. Maybe. But there's another consideration. We do know that once they got in the boat, they ran into a huge, life-threatening storm. Maybe these experienced fishermen could see it coming. Maybe they didn't relish the idea of setting sail at night into the teeth of a Galilean storm. I can just hear Jesus talking with Peter:

"Alright, men. Time to go home. Safe journey."

"Uhh, I don't think we should go."

"I don't recall asking what you thought, my man. It's time to go."

"But Master, with respect. You're excellent at woodwork and great at teaching, but the lake is not your area. We know this lake. See those clouds? Feel that wind? Major storm brewing."

"As I said, get into the boat and go home."

"But . . ."

"*Get into the boat.*"

The disciples had seen him rebuke demons. There had been that unforgettable incident when He had cleared the Temple of the moneychangers. They knew He could speak so forcefully that even the elements obeyed him. But they had never heard him be so commanding with them. They heard the tone of his voice and saw the set of his jaw, and they jumped in that boat and pulled on the oars with all their strength. Jesus the Lord had spoken.

Sometimes we forget Jesus is Lord. Sometimes He tells his people to get into boats they have no desire to board, and He compels them to set sail for destinations they have no desire to visit. He is the Lord

Jesus, and He issues orders. He didn't say, "Who would like to get in the boat?" He didn't inquire, "Who likes boats?" He certainly didn't offer options: "Those who don't mind getting wet, please board now. Those who are worried they might catch a cold, stay here with me."

Jesus wanted them in that boat because the lesson they were intended to learn through the feeding of the five thousand had gone right over their heads. They had totally missed the point. He needed to put them in a position where the point could be made all over again. That position, they would soon discover, was in a swamped boat in the middle of a raging storm. Not the most comfortable place for a learning experience.

But what was the lesson they had failed to learn a few hours earlier? When Jesus fed the immense crowd with five loaves and two fishes, He demonstrated a concept I like to put this way:

Human resources,
however limited,
when willingly offered
and divinely empowered,
are more than adequate
to achieve divine ends.

Our assets might be meager, but if we make them available to the Lord, He can do great things with them. That's a lesson that can change the course of a life.

So the reluctant disciples set sail, and Jesus was left alone. It had been a long day. He prayed well into the night. As He did, the wind picked up and the waves grew, and as dawn was breaking, He could just see the boat with his men struggling to stay afloat in the middle of the lake. All those hours and they still hadn't made it to the other side! They needed him. So He went to join them.

He walked, of course. Some people have a problem believing that this actually happened. If Jesus was just an ordinary man, then there's no reason to believe that He walked on water, and plenty of reasons to believe that He didn't. The psalmist, recounting the mighty acts of Jehovah, foretold, "Your path led through the sea, your way through the mighty waters, though your footprints were not seen" (Psalm 77:19). And Job added, "He alone stretches out the heavens and treads on the waves of the sea" (Job 9:8). So, far from being unbelievable, the action of Jesus striding across Galilee should be a faith builder — He really was who He said He was.

The twelve men in the boat had their own problems when they saw Jesus heading in their direction. "It's a ghost," they cried out in terror. Evidently their time with Jesus had not affected their native superstitions. This reaction on their part raises another interesting issue.

It is often said that "seeing is believing," and yet the opposite can be true. The Galileans didn't believe that men could walk on water — nobody is criticizing them for that. But they did believe in ghosts. So what happened when they saw someone walking on water? They "saw" a ghost. Their preconceived ideas precluded them from seeing reality, and allowed them to see only what they found acceptable. What they believed determined what they perceived. For them, believing was seeing. We're no different today.

Jesus called out to the men, "Take courage! It is I. Don't be afraid." Telling frightened people not to be afraid and admonishing them to be brave isn't usually helpful. But Jesus added something extra. He said, "It is I." This expression, literally translated from the original Greek, is actually "I AM"—the words that had been used from ancient days by Jehovah to describe himself. The title suggests that God is not limited as we are. He does not explain that last week He was, this week He is, and next week He will be. He just is. All the time. He is complete and entire in himself. He is "I am." They should not have been afraid simply because of who He was — and is.

Peter heard the "I AM" and shouted above the wind, "Can I come and join you, if it's really you?" On being given permission, he promptly jumped over the side — give him an "A" for reckless enthusiasm — and set out across the intervening space, his eyes firmly on Jesus. That is, until he realized what he had done. Taking his eyes off Jesus, he noticed the wind and the waves and started to sink. He cried out for help. "Save me!" His prayer of necessity was brief, but sincere.

Contrary to what we may believe, the effectiveness of prayer is not determined by volume, eloquence, or duration, but by its earnest sincerity and the ability of the Receiver of prayers to hear and answer. "Save me," Peter bellowed above the howling gale. He was heard; he was delivered. Jesus reached out his hand and saved Peter from drowning. Highly relieved, Peter no doubt wanted only to get back in the relative safety of the boat, but apparently the Lord wanted to grill him.

Jesus wanted to know, "Why did you start doubting? You were doing so well. Why didn't you keep your eyes on me? What happened?"

I don't know if Peter answered. I can just picture him, out there on the water trying to concentrate on giving a good answer, but mostly wanting to get out of the lake and out of the storm. The point was, Peter had made his meager resources available to the Lord — willingly, expectantly. Jesus had proved powerful enough to deal with the situation. In the power of the Lord, Peter walked on the water. But when he withdrew his focus from Jesus, Peter sank.

Jesus wanted his disciples to recognize that spiritual possibilities are not determined by human abilities, but by divine power. The big question is not "How much can we expect out of this unlikely disciple?" but rather "What can the Lord do with this unlikely, unpromising, ill-equipped but committed and expectant soul?"

The interview was mercifully brief. Peter and Jesus got back into the boat, which was brought safely to harbor, and the men returned to their families. Tired and wet, but challenged and amazed, they fell into bed. The new day was already dawning and the learning curve was getting steeper. There was much to be done and more lessons to learn.

The next morning there was a lot of activity on the lake. Boatloads of people began to arrive. The word had spread that free bread was on hand and miracles were happening. The crowds were in a hurry to catch the action.

But when they found Jesus, He was in no mood to satisfy their curiosity or to waste time on niceties. He bluntly pointed out to them that their interest in him was purely material and that the real issues He had come to address were apparently of little or no interest to them. They wanted to talk about material issues, but they needed to address spiritual matters. Their thoughts were firmly rooted in the here and now, while He wanted to introduce eternal issues. They only had stomachs for "food that spoils." Jesus wanted to tell them about "food that endures to life eternal."

The mention of eternal life provoked a response. In their minds, eternal life was a divine reward for good grades in life. So naturally, when He brought up the subject, they quizzed him on what it would take to merit the ultimate prize. His answer mystified them. They needed to believe. It wasn't a matter of doing; it was all about believing. That was something of a conundrum to them — and has been to multitudes ever since. He was telling them that eternal life is a gift, not a reward.

Their response was basically, "Alright, if you want us to believe in you, what sign will you give that will convince us you are worthy of our trust?" Apparently, they discounted the miracle of the multiplied loaves and fishes from the day before. It might have been enough of a miracle to satisfy you or me. But the rabbis taught that when Messiah came, He would be far superior to Moses, and He would do things that would make Moses' remarkable feats pale in significance. So if Jesus wanted to be taken seriously, He needed to do something really spectacular.

Moses had led thousands of Israelites out of the clutches of Pharaoh, organized them in the wilderness, and for forty years had tolerated their despicable behavior and fed them on a daily basis. Their Scriptures said Moses gave them "bread from heaven." The wilderness wanderers were not impressed. They persisted in calling it "manna," which means, "What is it?" For forty years Moses offered them "bread from heaven" and for the whole time they retorted, "What is it?" Their disdain for the provision and their dislike of the menu notwithstanding, the action of Moses was without precedent. And what had Jesus done so far? Well, He'd fed five thousand families — once. Not the kind of thing that would overshadow Moses' actions. Hardly the sort of sign that would give Jesus the credentials a skeptical crowd sought.

Peter held his breath. *These people have a point.* He wanted evidence, and the evidence he'd seen, while amazing, was not really up to the standards Scripture required. Jesus had done great things, but compared to Moses, they weren't great enough.

Jesus spoke, using the ancient "Amen, Amen" to alert his hearers that something of great significance was about to fall from his lips. "Moses didn't give you the bread from heaven." That was incredible. They all knew what Moses had done. Was He daring to revise history? To deny the undeniable? "It is my Father who gives you true bread."

He used the words "My Father" as if He could claim some special relationship to the Creator. There was a buzz of consternation in the crowd. He went on, "The real bread you need is not an ordinary loaf or even extraordinary manna, but a quality of life that will satisfy the yearnings of your hearts as surely as your daily bread meets the needs of your stomach." This saying rang a bell. Had not Moses said, "Man does not live on bread alone but on every word that comes from the mouth of the LORD" (Deuteronomy 8:3)? Was Jesus saying that He in some way was about to deliver a diet of spiritual nourishment that would satisfy for all time? "I am the bread of life," He proclaimed. "I am the bread that came down from heaven."

This was too much for the local people. They knew He was Jesus, the son of Joseph. They knew his family. They had watched him grow up. He had mended their plows and fixed their chairs. They were not about to accept that He had come down from heaven. The grumbling intensified, the murmuring increased, the tension began to build.

"You're all interested in eternal life. I'm here to tell you it's not a reward; it's a gift. And I'm the gift. I'm the bread you need to feed your eternal longings; I'm the diet you need to meet your daily needs. In the same way that you eat bread to satisfy your hunger, you will have to eat my flesh if you want eternal life."

This was outrageous. Eat his flesh? Disgusting. But there was worse to come. "And unless you drink my blood, you won't experience the life of which I'm speaking." Drink his blood? How dare He say such a thing? Every man in the crowd knew that Moses had spoken in the name of the Lord, "Any Israelite or any alien . . . who eats any blood — I will set my face against that person who eats blood and will cut him off from his people" (Leviticus 17:10). Was He defying Moses? Worse — was He contradicting God?

But Jesus was speaking in symbols. He had started talking about bread, moved to manna, then "bread from heaven," and arrived at his own flesh and blood as the bread from heaven. It was all about staple diets. Bread for ordinary life, manna for extraordinary life in a barren wilderness, and himself for life eternal. All three kinds of food were gifts from God. All had to be accepted by faith, received with gratitude, and eaten with thanksgiving. They had to receive him by faith and feed on him as surely as they partook of their daily bread.

But He had one final point up his sleeve. "You want a sign superior to what Moses gave you? Alright. Here's one. All the people Moses fed are dead, right? All the people who feed on me, who receive eternal life as a gift from me, will live forever. The best Moses could do was keep his thousands alive for a few years. I will keep you alive for all eternity."

You'd think that would capture their attention. But the people were not interested in eternal life. They were fixated on this life. They were not enthused about an eternal kingdom. They wanted a restored kingdom of Israel — now. They were into instant gratification, so they began to voice their disapproval. This was not the kind of teaching they wanted. Their itching ears desired something more practical and relevant. Jesus dealt in the practical and relevant, but He also dealt in the bigger issues, and now was one of those times. They were having none of it. They would look elsewhere for a prophet who would be more to their liking. So they left, in large numbers.

Jesus turned to his select group of twelve. I wish we knew the tone of voice in which He spoke. Was it with deep disappointment? Was He compassionate? Or could it have been in a steely and challenging voice that He said, "You do not want to leave, too, do you?"

Peter, who had listened intently to the teaching and whose

emotions had been on a roller-coaster journey, spoke up, "Where could we go, Lord? You're the one who has the words of eternal life. You're the Holy One of God."

Subsequent events would show that Peter's growing appreciation of Jesus still had holes in it. But in the face of mass desertion, he stood his ground. In the midst of the crass materialistic thinking of his contemporaries, he kept his focus on things eternal. When all around him people grumbled at Jesus, Peter had nothing but praise for him. The Rock was standing firm. This was one of his finest moments. Definite signs of growth in the man.

Peter and his friends had a golden opportunity to cut their losses, accept the fact that they had backed a loser, and go home sadder but wiser. Jesus even asked them if that was what they planned to do, but Peter came through. Not because he understood all that he was hearing, and certainly not because he agreed with everything that was going on. But he did know enough to know truth when he heard it and reality when he saw it. And that was enough for him.

It should be enough for us, too. As we confront the imponderables of life and face up to the questions that yield no easy answers, there should be enough comfort and conviction in the company of Jesus to hold us fast.

Today there is a pervasive loss of confidence in the truth of the Bible. Disillusionment with the church's leadership. Plummeting moral standards. The fatal attraction of a fast-paced culture and the insistence on instant gratification. These factors have all contributed to dramatic fallout, minimal commitment, and marginal involvement in the contemporary church. We need unlikely pillars, unmovable anchors. Steadfast people. People who, like Peter, know their faults and failings, but also know where truth is found. When everyone around you is looking somewhere else for what they want to hear, where will you be?

BRAVE ENOUGH TO THINK ABOUT IT

1. *Success in any endeavor — including Christian ministry — can lead to devastating pride.* After their triumphant first mission trip, the disciples were excited about their newfound power. But Jesus seemed to be cautious about their attitude and decided they needed to take a break, relax, and reflect on all that had happened. He saw that they were impressed with what they had done and were beginning to lose sight of the true source of their authority.

   a. What's wrong with being excited about your success? What was Jesus worried about in the disciples' attitudes?

   b. Why do we need to continually give the credit to God? Aren't there times when we can just be happy we've succeeded and leave it at that?

   c. Think of a time when you were proud of an accomplishment. Did you cross the line into foolish pride? Or did you praise God and give him the glory?

2. *God gives us strength and energy to continue doing his work, even when we're weary.* Jesus was tired and grieving, but when He saw the great need of the people, He was energized to help them. Likewise, we can draw on his strength when we think we have nothing left to give. The key is that we trust him — and we have to make sure we're doing his work. (He might not be forthcoming with the extra energy just so we can put in a ninety-hour workweek and look good to the boss.)

   a. What kind of situation in your own life might this principle apply to? What areas of your life could improve if you were to trust God more for strength and energy?

   b. Have you ever found yourself saying things such as, "I would do more in ministry, but I'm just too busy with my job and my family"? How can the principle of drawing on Christ's strength help to change this pattern?

   c. How do we know the difference between doing God's work and doing our own work?

3. *Our limited resources, when willingly offered and divinely empowered, are more than adequate to achieve God's purposes.* More than once, Jesus fed thousands of people with a few meager morsels that had been freely offered to him. He was always working with the limited resources people had to offer, but achieving his purposes nonetheless. He wants us to get out of the mode of thinking we don't have "enough" to share, and trust him to stretch our resources so that we'll still have enough, even after we've given some away.

   a. What specific resources do you have that you think are too limited for you to share freely with others? Your time? Your money? Your love? Why?

   b. How does this principle apply to your tithing and charitable giving? How can God multiply your meager contributions in order to accomplish his great works?

   c. What would it be like to offer your whole self to God to use for his purposes? Could you do this? How would you do it?

4. *In following Jesus, we need to keep our eyes on him. Taking our eyes off him, diverting our attention to the world around us, leads to doubt.* When Peter stepped out of the boat, he did so in complete trust, based on who he knew Jesus to be. He didn't think about the impossibility of walking on water; he only thought about who Jesus was — and he stayed above the waves. The moment Peter lost his focus on Jesus, he saw the wind and waves and doubted the reality of what he was doing. He sank.

   a. Why did Peter start to sink when he noticed the wind and the waves? Why does the world around us cause us to doubt Christ?

   b. What times in your life have you focused on the Lord and accomplished seemingly impossible things? If this has never happened, what do you think the reason is?

   c. What events and circumstances have caused you to doubt God? What specific things have you questioned in your doubting? How did those doubts affect your ability to function in your normal day-to-day life?

5. *We are often so focused on material needs and the "here and now" that we ignore larger spiritual truths.* The crowds of people hung around Jesus as long as He seemed to have something to give — something tangible and immediately gratifying. Once they realized He was switching gears and wanted to talk about more important eternal matters, they departed in droves. Like them, we might be paying lip service to "spiritual matters" when really, we just want God to make sure our bills are paid, heal our disease, and prevent our house from burning down.

   a. Do you think Jesus is only concerned about eternal, spiritual things, or does He deal in the material, tangible realm as well? Defend your answer using Scripture and evidence from your own life.

   b. Why is it difficult to move beyond worrying about physical, material needs, and focus on more important eternal issues? How much do you really care about the spiritual, ephemeral issues? Do they impact your day-to-day experience?

   c. What strategies could you use to help yourself focus more on eternal matters?

BRAVE ENOUGH FOR ACTION

It's easy enough to talk about how Jesus can achieve his purposes using our meager resources. It's another story to actually put it into practice. Here's a challenge: Set aside a certain amount of money — whatever amount makes sense to you. (It should be enough that you feel it, but not so much that you'll default on your mortgage. Perhaps $100.) Commit to use this money to advance God's kingdom. Begin praying about how the Lord wants you to use this money. Take your time thinking about it and praying about it. Ask God to show you how to use the money in a way that will multiply and bring glory to him. Begin looking around for people and situations that need help — your possible opportunities for giving. When the time is right, use the money in the way that you are led and watch what happens. Are you surprised at how much your small sum accomplished? Was God glorified in the transaction?

chapter 5

SINCERELY WRONG

MATTHEW 16:13-26
LUKE 9:22-25

*J*esus decided it was time to take his message to the region
around the city of Caesarea Philippi, so He and his party
headed north. As the evangelistic band made its way around the villages, Jesus used the traveling time for informal instruction. "Who
do people say the Son of Man is?" He asked on one occasion. "Son
of Man" was his favorite way of referring to himself.

The people gave various answers concerning the identity of Jesus.
But Jesus had more in mind than an inquiry into popular opinion.
His next question was penetrating and direct, addressed to the
Twelve: "But what about you? Who do you say I am?" Apparently
He had decided that the disciples had been exposed to him long
enough to form an opinion as to his identity, and He expected them
to articulate their convictions.

"You are the Christ, the Son of the living God," Peter confidently
stated. Whatever Peter thought he meant by these words, Jesus
affirmed that he was right. But He also pointed out that Peter had
not figured this out on his own. The Father in heaven had blessed

the fisherman with a special revelation. But what was so important about what Peter had said?

To say that Jesus was the Christ was to state that He was the long-promised and deeply desired deliverer, the Messiah who would come and set things right for God's beleaguered people. Ever since God's covenant with Abraham, there had been an element of hope and expectation in the hearts of God's people. They had always looked for better days ahead. Over the centuries more than a few men had arisen, claiming to be the Messiah. One by one they had crashed and burned and taken the trust of the people with them. But hope was not dead, certainly not in Peter's heart. Now aided by divine insight, he proclaimed loudly that Jesus was the Christ.

Not only did Peter declare that Jesus was the long-awaited Messiah, he added that Jesus was "the Son of the living God." At different points in Scripture the term is applied to kings or angels, but in this case there are definite connotations of deity. Later, after Jesus was arrested and was being questioned by the authorities, He would be asked, "Are you then the Son of God?" His affirmative answer would be an unmistakable claim to deity that the authorities wouldn't tolerate, and for which they would sentence him to death.

Peter was hardly giving a well-thought-out and carefully articulated statement of his convictions. He was responding to a remarkable insight that had been graciously given to him by the Father. As we are all inclined to do, Peter put this revelation through the filter of his own misconceptions, and though he stated the truth, he still had no idea what that truth meant. Jesus told him, "Blessed are you,

Simon son of John, for this was not revealed to you by man, but by my Father in heaven."

But Jesus had more to say. He referred to the new name He had given Peter — the Rock — and stated that, true to his name, Peter would be a rock *(petra)*, unique and profoundly valuable to the cause of Christ. "I tell you that you are Peter, and on this rock I will build my church and the gates of Hades will not overcome it," He said to the startled disciples.

If the disciples on the road to Caesarea Philippi were startled, the disciples of Jesus on the road ever since have wrestled with this statement — and frequently with each other — over the exact meaning of Jesus' words. But before we look into the differences of understanding, we should note the things He said that should bring great joy and confidence and purpose.

Jesus promised to build his church. It was going to be *his* church and He was going to accept responsibility for seeing that it was built. Not only that, He promised that death itself would not overcome it. It would be a church that would triumph over adversity, survive all ills, and fulfill his eternal purposes. He would build it and nothing and no one would stop him.

Clearly the calling of Peter to become the Rock was unique. Peter was foundational, and you don't keep on building foundations. But you do build superstructures on them, and this is where we come into the equation. We may not be the Rock, but Jesus is still looking for bricks. Far too many people think of church as somewhere they go — or don't go — whereas Jesus showed that church is something we are.

This was the first time Jesus had mentioned building a church. His disciples knew that a church — an *ekklesia* — was literally a "called-out people," so they would have understood that Jesus planned to develop some kind of community to which his followers would belong. Anyone claiming to be Messiah could certainly be expected to establish an *ekklesia*. Why then was his statement startling?

Previously, Jesus' teaching had been focused on "the kingdom" that He had come to establish. But it was becoming increasingly clear that opposition to Jesus was building rapidly, and that the kingdom He was advocating differed dramatically from the one envisioned by the people of his day. Jesus had never intended to limit his "kingdom" to Israel, and the time had come to broaden the picture. He wanted his people to begin to embrace the idea of a community of believers that would transcend Israel and would eventually incorporate people from "all the nations" who would be blessed through Israel, exactly as God had promised Abraham. The Israel of Peter's day had forgotten that they were blessed in Abraham in order that through them, all the nations of the world would be blessed. Now it was going to happen — and they had to get ready. Jesus was giving notice that, while his initial followers would come from Israel, very soon the community of believers committed to him would be made up of people coming from far beyond Israel's borders. This new community would be called the church — the called-out people.

The vision had been expanded, and in time the disciples would grasp the enormity of Jesus' project — the realities of the expansion.

The church would transcend racial, ethnic, and national boundaries. His kingdom, unlike the kingdoms of the Assyrians, the Babylonians, and the Greeks, would not pass away. Even Rome was beginning to decline and fall. But not his kingdom. The church would never die.

"This is what I have in mind," He told them. "This is what I'm going to build. Nothing will stop me."

But what about Jesus' startling statement that his church would relate to Peter in some unique way? The Peter they knew so well. What could Jesus have possibly meant when He said, "You are Peter (*Petros*) and on this rock (*petra*) I will build my church"? We can only speculate on their puzzlement, but we don't need to guess about the debate that continues to this day.

Some segments of the church have seen this as a clear statement of Peter's primacy, and upon this idea have built a formidable body of belief. Put in the simplest of terms, they teach that Peter was the first Pope, the first in an unbroken line of succession in which unique gifts are exclusively preserved, passed on from generation to generation for the perpetuation of the church.

In reaction to this view, other segments of the church insist that the rock on which Jesus would build the church was not Peter at all, but rather the confession that he made. In other words, the church is all about people who, like Peter, recognize who Jesus is and gladly confess him as Lord and Savior.

Right now we're not going to delve into these long-standing differences, but it's my view that Jesus said that Peter, not his confession, was the rock on which the church would be built. However, this belief doesn't necessarily lead to the papal interpretation of Peter's role. There can be no doubt that Peter was the first to be called to discipleship. Peter made the first confession of Jesus as Messiah, Son of the living God, a foundational statement. Peter was the "take charge" person more than once, contributing greatly to the early development of the community of believers. It was he who would open the door on the day of Pentecost when thousands would flood into the kingdom. It was Peter who would eventually open the door of faith to the Gentiles. There is much evidence that Jesus did begin to build his church on Peter.

But Jesus said more to Peter that day. "I will give you the keys of the kingdom of heaven," He said. What does this mean?

Jesus had spoken strongly to the Pharisees about their failure to teach the people. He said, "You have taken away the key to knowledge. You yourselves have not entered, and you have hindered those who were entering" (Luke 11:52). In marked contrast to this failure, Jesus was now entrusting Peter with the task of giving people the opportunity to enter the new community of belief that would last into eternity.

Jesus went on, "Whatever you bind on earth will be bound in heaven, and whatever you loose on earth will be loosed in heaven." Startling words. They suggest power the like of which no man has ever possessed. Would Jesus really entrust such far-reaching power to a man? The power to shut up or open heaven? The power to make earthly actions binding for eternity and temporal decisions relevant forever? Surely not. But even if He did, would He really entrust that kind of power to Peter, of all people?

Two things need to be said on this score. First, a careful study of this passage leads me to understand that Jesus did not give Peter the power to grant or deny access to the kingdom, but that the way of access or denial had already been decided in heaven. Jesus was saying that Peter and his colleagues could say on the authority of heaven, "If you acknowledge Jesus as Lord, you'll inherit the kingdom. If you don't, you won't." Their spoken words would be endorsed in heaven — the angelic hosts would nod enthusiastically in agreement.

This must have been the high point of Peter's life. Not only had he discovered the Messiah — that was the greatest thing a Jewish man could possibly hope for — but he had been the first to announce his arrival, and now Jesus was promising him great things. Regrettably, Peter's triumph was short-lived.

Jesus immediately told the disciples, "Do not say a word about this. Your lips must be sealed. I forbid you to tell anyone that I am the Christ, the Son of God."

This made no sense at all to Peter. *Why must I keep quiet? Doesn't everybody need to know what we've discovered?* Messiah had come, presumably, to be recognized, honored, and followed. How could Jesus possibly function as Messiah if nobody knew who He was?

The depth of Peter's misunderstanding and the seriousness of his error quickly came to the surface as Jesus began to teach them what being Messiah was all about. "The Son of Man must suffer many things," Jesus began to explain. He seemed to place special emphasis on the "must." This was perfectly in line with what the prophet Isaiah had announced years earlier, "It was the LORD's will to crush him and cause him to suffer" (Isaiah 53:10). But the Jews understood this prophecy to relate to God's servant Israel, not to Messiah. In Peter's mind, Jesus was not going to suffer, He was going to succeed. He had not the slightest understanding that Jesus' success as Messiah was directly related to the depth of his suffering.

Jesus went on to explain that his sufferings would begin at the hands of the "elders, chief priests and teachers of the law." Peter must have been dumbfounded. *To be rejected by these power brokers will guarantee your failure!* Any would-be Messiah needed to be embraced and endorsed by the authorities. To say that He would suffer this kind of rejection was, in Peter's mind, either serious political miscalculation, or total disqualification for the role of Messiah. Peter was getting worried. *Does Jesus know what He's talking about?*

Jesus then explained the nature of his great rejection. He told his men bluntly that He would be killed. Not crowned — killed. Again, He stressed the "must." He was not just saying that He would die, or even predicting that He would be murdered, but insisting that his dying was necessary. It was part of the plan. It was what being Messiah meant.

This is too much.

Peter tried to protest but Jesus calmly went on to say the most stunning words yet: "After three days I will rise again." No doubt Peter's views of death and afterlife were, like those of many of his contemporaries, confused and vague. So it is no wonder that Peter was deeply troubled by the things Jesus was saying.

By Peter's reckoning, Jesus was absolutely mistaken. *He has to be corrected. I can't keep quiet about this.* Because Peter had the insight to recognize Messiah, he surely had the ability to correct Messiah. He would not shirk his duty. He would halt Jesus' confused and confusing rambling before it went any further. *Jesus must be stopped before He spreads any more alarm among the disciples.*

Unable to control his frustration a moment longer, Peter took Jesus by the arm, led him a short distance away, and burst out with surprising vehemence, "Absolutely not! How dare you think in these terms. This is totally unacceptable."

If it seems unlikely that Peter talked to his Master in such a manner, note that Matthew and Mark both use the word "rebuke" to describe the way Peter spoke to Jesus (see Matthew 16:22; Mark 8:32). Peter was adamant. He strenuously objected to what Jesus was saying.

Jesus listened to Peter's angry rebuke and then, turning to include all the other disciples, He reprimanded Peter in no uncertain terms: "Out of my sight, Satan!"

Jesus had never said such words to his disciples. They had heard his words of encouragement and comfort, of grace and forgiveness, of reproof and correction. But never had they heard such words from his lips, other than when He found it necessary to challenge the forces of evil blatantly lined up against him. He talked that way to demons — but not disciples.

Peter was stunned. *Did He just call me Satan?* The disciples were horrified. Like whipped puppies, they backed away from his presence, furtively glancing at each other, scarcely daring to look at the strong countenance of their suddenly stern leader.

Perhaps Peter, in his well-documented enthusiasm and newly discovered status, had overstepped the mark in rebuking Jesus. His social graces were suspect. If he thought it, he said it. If he believed it, he proclaimed it. *If you have something to say, you should say it.* Surely Jesus could have made some allowances for Peter's excess of enthusiasm. Maybe Peter had been wrong to speak as he did, but at least he was sincere. Sincerely wrong, as it happened.

But Jesus' response was not an angry reaction to Peter's rough and ready rebuke. The Master was in complete control of his emotions. The application of Satan's name to Peter's person was well-considered and carefully articulated. He knew the disciples needed an explanation, even if they were unlikely to understand it at the time. So He added, "You do not have in mind the things of God, but the things of men."

In other words, they were looking at Jesus' approach to Messiahship from a purely human point of view, without any perception of the divine intentions behind Messiah's mission. In one sense, they could hardly be blamed for looking at things from a human point of view because they were human. But Peter had just received divine insight that had enabled him to recognize Messiah. Perhaps he should have been able to recognize the truthfulness of Jesus' explanation of his mission. At least, he should have listened with respectful silence. If he'd needed clarification, he could have asked. But none of these considerations explained Jesus calling Peter "Satan." Why had Jesus used such devastating language?

The evil plan of Satan is simply to thwart the purposes of God. The purpose of God in sending his Son into the world was that He should intentionally die on a cross as a substitutionary sacrifice for the sins of the world. Satan knew this, and was endeavoring to stop Jesus from going to Jerusalem, where He would be rejected and crucified and rise again. Satan wanted to stop Jesus from going to the cross; Peter wanted to stop Jesus from going to the cross. Without knowing it, and for widely different reasons, Peter found himself in league with Satan. Satan's plans were malicious; Peter's ideas were benevolent. Satan desired to thwart God's grand cosmic plan; Peter wanted only to further what he thought God's plan for Israel should be. Satan was playing on Peter's highly tuned emotions like a concert violinist.

Poor Peter. In the space of a single day he had gone from the mountaintop of spiritual experience to the depths of despair. Such a stinging rebuke from Jesus would probably have destroyed a lesser man than Peter. From a purely human point of view, if Peter had packed his bags and headed home, no one would have been surprised. There is only so much humiliation a man can take. But Peter, true to form, was a rock. Perhaps the next words of Jesus penetrated his wounded spirit.

Jesus took the opportunity to explain that the path to blessedness often leads through suffering. This was the way Jesus would procure salvation for a lost humanity. If the disciples identified with him, the suffering Messiah, they must not assume they would be exempt from suffering. Jesus did not reserve this teaching on suffering for his committed disciples — He shared it with the uncommitted, too. Speaking to the entire crowd, He said, "If anyone would come after me, he must deny himself and take up his cross and follow me."

He was saying that anyone who desires to be his follower must follow him the whole way — even through suffering. But He was also promising that He'd lead. He would always show the way through pain, and his followers would always have him as an example. He went on to explain that anyone who wanted to have real life would first have to lose their own lives for his sake. He was giving a complete picture of "follow-ship." It could not be a halfway effort. A disciple would have to follow him all the way, no matter what the price.

Our human tendency is to desire blessing without cost, solutions to problems without delay, and the fulfillment of desires without inconvenience. In our culture, desires have in many cases developed into rights, and when these "rights" are not met, resentment sets in. This resentment is directed at God, who in some strange human equation is required to bless as demanded and retire gracefully into irrelevance once He has delivered. Should He fail to do so, He is dismissed into oblivion or treated with disdain.

In the Western world we are so blessed with a thousand ways of dulling our pain that we tend to see suffering as an unwarranted intrusion. Its elimination becomes our obsession. Someone has said that the difference between the people of the West and the East is that the former say, "Get this pain off my back," while the latter say, "Strengthen my back to bear this pain." Peter was not a Westerner.

Neither was Jesus, and having administered the painful rebuke, He promptly began to work to strengthen his disciple by explaining that suffering was an integral dimension of his ministry and would be an inevitable part of the life of his followers. In the same way that salvation would not be possible without a cross, so discipleship would not be viable without a cost.

Coming to grips with this fundamental dimension of discipleship is profoundly difficult for those of us who have been raised in a culture that will do anything to avoid pain and embrace pleasure. The challenge therefore is, how do we cope when trouble comes? How do we respond when the call to sacrificial living sounds in our hearts? Do we grow resentful, wondering why this is happening to us? Do we protest that because salvation is free — which it is — discipleship should be without cost — which it isn't? Do we embrace suffering and sacrifice with confidence that a gracious Lord will work in and through the circumstances to his glory and our ultimate good? The answer to those questions will determine whether or not we progress in the growth pattern of life in Christ or plateau and begin a slow slide into spiritual decline.

Numbed and hurt as he was, Peter could see through the mist of his pain that Jesus' prediction of suffering was not unrealistic. Was not the history of Israel one long saga of struggle and conflict? *Why should it be any different now?* Jesus' warning that his followers should expect suffering was also reasonable.

Maybe I should stick around a little longer. True, Peter didn't agree with what Jesus was saying. Surely there were better ways of doing things. And equating him with Satan still seemed too severe. But Peter was a resilient character. He would sort that out later with Jesus. This whole business about resurrection had him totally perplexed, but there was no point running away until he had some more answers. So Peter, brave soul, licked his wounds and doggedly followed the group — but not quite up front as usual. A respectful distance was called for, and he took it.

Brave Enough to Think About It

1. *If we, like Peter, acknowledge Jesus as Lord and Savior, we will also be a part of Christ's building his church.* Peter is the foundation, but we're all important stones in the edifice. The church isn't a building, but a worldwide "called-out" community of believers.

   a. Why is it important for you to regularly confess to Jesus, "You are the Christ"? Do you do it? Why does it sometimes seem like "just words," and how can you avoid that?

   b. If Jesus could build his eternal church on Peter and his acknowledgment of him as Lord, what can He build on you and your acknowledgment of who He is?

   c. How does your view of "church" differ from Christ's? Will your perspective change now that you know how He sees it? Why or why not?

   d. What does it mean to be a stone in Christ's church? How is He using you to continue building?

2. *The Christian life often includes suffering, and the road to our spiritual transformation isn't always smooth.* When we try to circumvent this reality, we're thinking "our way," not God's way. The symbol of Christianity is a cross. The secret of Christian living is the willingness to carry the cross and to rely on Christ for the strength to bear the pain, rather than begging him to take it away.

   a. Being as honest as possible, consider: How do you respond to Christ's call to "carry a cross"? Do you embrace it? Reject it? Try to ignore it?

   b. What do you think it means, in contemporary twenty-first century life, to carry a cross? Have you experienced it? If your life is going along smoothly with no major problems, how can you carry a cross?

   c. How can you be a true follower of Christ if you don't experience suffering because of him?

3. *Even in the midst of our best intentions, Satan can use us for evil.* Sometimes, you and Satan might have the same goal, but for different reasons. For instance, you might desire to avoid suffering, and Satan might want the same for you in order to further his own ambitions. But Christ has the power to stop Satan in his tracks.

   a. What are some common life goals you've had that, when looked at more carefully, might be Satan's plans for you, not Christ's? What might Satan be hoping to accomplish in your life through these goals?

   b. How can you tell the difference between God's desires for you and Satan's? How would you recognize the evil one's influence?

   c. If you were to realize that Satan was using you for his purposes, how could you stop him?

   d. Is our culture more under the influence of Christ or Satan? Defend your answer. How does this impact your life?

4. *When Christ humbles us, it is an opportunity to choose between pride (ourselves) and submission (himself).* Peter received an incredible compliment from the Lord — that his declaration was correct and that he would be the "Rock." Immediately, pride began to grow in Peter, and he thought he was worthy to correct Jesus' teaching about suffering. Peter then received the sternest rebuke possible from Jesus.

   a. When has your pride caused you to go down a wrong road? How long did it take you to figure it out and correct it?

   b. Why was it necessary for Jesus to rebuke Peter like that? After such a humbling experience, would you have stuck with Jesus or headed home?

   c. Think of a time you were humbled by another person. What was your reaction? Have you ever been humbled by a revelation from God? How did you respond? Compare these two experiences.

BRAVE ENOUGH FOR ACTION

Peter's confession of Jesus as "the Christ, the Son of the living God" was a major turning point in his own life, as well as in the bigger picture of the gospel story. Sometimes the fact that Jesus is the Son of God seems rather obvious to us, and it's hard to understand why that declaration was so pivotal. If you would like a better understanding of its importance, try this exercise: Commit to spend twenty minutes each day for a week meditating on the theme of Peter's confession. Begin your session by reading a passage. (Use Matthew 16:13-20; Mark 8:27-30; or Luke 9:18-20.) Picture yourself in the situation. Think about what it would have been like to have Jesus ask you the question. Pray for God to give you his wisdom and any revelations He wants you to have. Reflect on what the confession meant for Peter and what it means for you. Make the declaration yourself. Write down any new thoughts, revelations, or new understandings you have. After doing this for several days, do you have a deeper appreciation for Peter's momentous confession?

HARD TO BE HUMBLE

MATTHEW 17—18
LUKE 9:28-45

No leader who cares about his followers enjoys rebuking them, as no loving father likes disciplining an erring son. But leaders and fathers know that correction, reproof, and rebuke are as necessary as encouragement, affirmation, and support for the ones in their care to become who they are destined to be. The leader who fails to apply correction when necessary fails to provide leadership when needed. But what comes after the showdown? Where does the leader go with his follower? Is rebuke all that is needed? Great care is needed in the time following a serious reprimand, for mistakes can be made and damage done precisely at this point.

In some instances, the tension between leader and follower becomes so great, and the damage to their relationship so devastating, that they can no longer be in each other's presence. So they go their separate ways. The hours invested in the relationship go to waste, the lessons learned are rejected, the progress achieved is all for naught. Tragedy.

At the other extreme, a leader may administer a rebuke, but on seeing the pain it causes, immediately regret it, retract the perfectly appropriate reprimand, make amends, and allow the follower to proceed uncorrected and liable to repeat his mistake. Another tragedy.

How did Jesus handle his erring Rock? He neither cut him off nor did He immediately patch things up. He gave Peter some space. Time to think, time to heal, time to regain his equilibrium, time to process the new realities concerning suffering and discipleship.

Matthew, Mark, and Luke all carefully point out that Jesus allowed six to eight days to elapse before He made a specific approach to Peter (see Matthew 17:1; Mark 9:2; Luke 9:28). He was going to show Peter that he hadn't been sidelined. And He was going to give him a further revelation that would help him to understand the mystery of Christ's Messiah-ship.

"Peter," Jesus called out one morning, "find James and John. I want to show you something." Peter was apprehensive at first, but at least he would not be facing Jesus alone. His old friends would be with him.

Jesus had previously picked out this threesome for special treatment on the occasion of the raising of the twelve-year-old daughter of a prominent synagogue ruler. The man's name was Jairus and he'd earnestly begged Jesus to come and heal his little girl. Jesus agreed to accompany the distraught man, but was held up when a woman with a bleeding disorder touched his robes in the crowd. Even though He was being jostled and pushed by all the people, Jesus had been aware of her longing for help and her great faith, and had sensed that healing power had flowed from himself into her. Peter was mystified, but there was no doubt that the woman's condition was immediately healed. Then some of Jairus' servants came rushing into the crowd and announced that the girl had died and there was no need to trouble Jesus any further. But Jesus took Peter, James, and John with him, went to the child's house, and brought her back to life.

Peter was well aware that he and his two friends were privileged. He was encouraged that this latest invitation seemed to indicate that his value hadn't been totally destroyed by the events at Caesaria Phillipi. *At least I hope so.*

Jesus set out purposefully toward the foothills. "Where are we going, Master?" the disciples asked as they hurried to keep up with him.

"You'll see. Now save your breath. It's all uphill from here." Onward and upward the men toiled in the heat of the day until finally they arrived on the summit of one of Israel's mountains. We're not sure which one, but traditionally, we're told it was Mount Tabor in the Valley of Jezreel. At less than 2,000 feet above sea level, it doesn't seem to fit Matthew and Mark's description of a "high mountain" (Matthew 17:1; Mark 9:2), leading some to believe they actually climbed Mount Hermon.

Jesus moved away from Peter, James, and John, and abruptly "His face shone like the sun, and his clothes became as white as the light" (Matthew 17:2). It was as if Jesus were being changed into another form — which is what "transfiguration" means — before their very eyes. Years later Peter wrote, "We were eyewitnesses of his majesty" (2 Peter 1:16), referring to this experience. John also recorded his recollections of the unforgettable event, writing, "We have seen his

glory, the glory of the One and Only, who came from the Father"
(John 1:14). Peter and his friends were seeing glory and majesty that
rightly belonged to the Son of God, which during the days of his
incarnation were necessarily veiled from human view by his humanity. But Jesus wanted these men to be assured that He truly was
Messiah, the Promised One, the Son of God from on high, so He
gave them a brief, unforgettable glimpse of the reality of who He
was. His deity burst through the confines of his humanity. They saw
it and were dazzled by it and were never the same again.

But there was more to come. As their eyes adjusted to the sight,
they perceived other figures conversing with Jesus. Moses and Elijah
were deep in conversation with the Master. How the Galileans
recognized these Old Testament heroes, we're not told. They had no
photographs. The men were not wearing name tags. But without a
doubt, they were Moses, the man who represented the Law, and
Elijah, the representative prophet.

Peter crept closer to hear what was being said. The law giver and
the prophet were discussing with Jesus details of "his departure,
which he was about to bring to fulfillment at Jerusalem" (Luke 9:31).
The literal translation is "the exodus He would accomplish."

Peter had already been told by Jesus that He would die and rise
again, and he had famously rejected the predictions. But now he
heard on no less authority than that of Moses and Elijah that Jesus
was about to leave and He would do it triumphantly.

Peter was receiving more than his fair share of revelation at this
point. First the glory, then the appearance of the great figures of

history, then the intimate conversation and the indications that Jesus' predictions were being endorsed by Moses and Elijah. *What does it mean?*

Peter had experienced many amazing things during his time with the Master — but do you ever get used to it? He was being forced again and again to reconsider exactly who Jesus was and what He was doing here.

But Peter was not given to much reflection. He was a man of action. He operated on intuition and impulse. So characteristically he said, "Lord, it is good for us to be here; if you wish, I will make three dwellings here, one for you, one for Moses and one for Elijah." The humiliation of the "Satan" incident was forgotten, the excitement of the new day took over, and Peter was once again his confident self: energetic, enthusiastic — and wrong. Even as he was outlining his proposal to hang on to the wonder of the moment, he and the others were enveloped in a brilliant cloud. The words died in his throat as a voice from the cloud boomed, "This is my Son, whom I love; with him I am well pleased. Listen to him!"

The voice, the cloud, the magnitude of the moment knocked Peter and his friends flat on their faces. They knew whose voice they were hearing, and Peter sensed he was once again receiving a rebuke. As if on cue, Moses and Elijah disappeared, the three disciples staggered to their feet, and Jesus alone stood there. The Son in whom the Father was well pleased. But Jesus' first thought was for his frightened men. "Get up. Don't be afraid," He told them. With that, He started down the mountain, followed by three bewildered Galileans.

On the way down, He told them once again that they were to remain silent about what they had seen and heard. But only until He had risen from the dead. Then they must speak out. *Why the delay?* If they talked about the remarkable transfiguration they had witnessed and the voice of God they'd heard, the people would be eager to respond to Jesus as Messiah — but it would not be a redemptive Messiah. The people's ideas of Messiah did not include any concept of death and resurrection any more than Peter's had. They would gladly embrace a cross-less Christ. But such a Christ had no place in the Father's eternal plan. Jesus had stated it clearly and unambiguously — the Son of Man must suffer.

Descending to the valley, the three disciples were full of questions. All this talk about Jesus being killed and the "departure" He would accomplish made no sense to them. They had no understanding of "rising from the dead" either. They were ready to consider — rather than reject outright — Jesus' words about being killed, but they had no understanding of the significance. The words made no sense. But they wouldn't forget the remarkable experience on the mountain where they had been witnesses to incontrovertible evidence that Jesus of Nazareth was Messiah, the Son of God. Of that they had no doubts.

Centuries before when Moses descended from the mountain in Sinai after his encounter with God, his face was radiant and everyone noticed, but he was totally unaware of it. We're not told if the disciples radiated anything of the glory to which they had been exposed, but it's reasonable to assume that some mention would have been made if their faces were shining. We can only surmise that something of the experience stayed in their hearts and minds once they arrived in the valley.

As is so often the case, after the ecstasy of the mountaintop experience, harsh reality came rushing in rudely and unbidden, in the shape of a troubled parent seeking healing for an epileptic son. The disciples who hadn't been to the mountaintop had tried to deal with the situation, but were unable to effect a cure. Jesus solved the problem by exorcising a demon that was contributing to the boy's condition. Then to their deep chagrin, the disciples heard Jesus express disappointment not only with them, but with the whole "unbelieving and perverse generation." To their embarrassment, they heard his frustration and irritation when He added, "How long shall I stay with you? How long shall I put up with you?" Perhaps his recent experience of his familiar eternal glory, now shrouded by his incarnation, had made him homesick for heaven.

Jesus' obvious displeasure certainly got the attention of his men. Conscious of their failure to do what they had been specifically commissioned and equipped to do, they asked him, with reference to the demon, "Why could we not cast him out?" They really wanted to know how and why they had failed. Jesus was more than happy to enlighten them.

The problem was the poor quality of their faith. This was apparent in their approach to prayer. They were aware that life is full of difficulties that loom like mountains, but they had to learn that these "mountains" are movable if approached in trusting, believing prayer that calls on the Lord to intervene according to his eternal purposes. This does not require great, spectacular steps of faith. Jesus said that faith as small as a mustard seed will be sufficient to release the power of God into a problematic situation.

In this particular case, it appears that the disciples, having been commissioned and equipped to deal with demons, had become casual and self-sufficient rather than earnest and dependent. Maybe they had fallen into the trap of believing that they themselves had what it takes to deal with demonic forces. The reality was that they were desperately dependent and conspicuously impotent in their own strength. They learned this lesson the hard way. In full view of an expectant public, their inadequacy was so obviously demonstrated that they even recognized it themselves.

But Jesus did not simply rebuke them and instruct them. He gave them a promise that they could latch on to and cling to for the rest of their days. "If you have faith as small as a mustard seed . . . nothing will be impossible for you" (Matthew 17:20). This did not mean that every problem would be promptly dismissed through believing prayer. But rather, that every problem that was standing in the way of them accomplishing what they had been specifically commissioned and equipped to do would be removed, so that the work of the kingdom might progress and triumph.

And so in the course of a few hours, Peter had been encouraged by the invitation to the mountain, enlightened by the dramatic display of Jesus' glory, foolishly shallow in his enthusiastic suggestions, perplexed in his questioning, publicly embarrassed by spiritual impotence, and exhilarated by the promise of future possibilities. He'd been to the mountain and descended to the valley. All in a day.

The huge truth that Peter faced, and the rest of us must face, resides in the valley beneath the mountaintop. We can go through worship experiences of intense emotion and ecstasy, but we cannot ignore the human suffering and devilish activity all around us. There is a connection between the mountaintop and valley experiences. It is in the power of the One we worship on the mountain that we are equipped to function in the valley.

But all too often there is a disconnect. Like Jesus' team members, we look back to our previous successes and become careless about the source of power, confident in our skills and experience, and eventually as ineffective as the disciples were. The disciples had the grace and humility to admit there was something lacking. They wanted to know why. So Jesus told them. Fortunately, we have seen their mistakes, and smart people learn from mistakes. Too bad for Peter, though. He had more mistakes ahead of him for us to learn from.

On the journey back to Capernaum, Jesus returned to the subject that had caused such problems in Caesarea Phillipi. This time around, Peter wisely kept his thoughts to himself. It appears that his mind was gradually being enlightened to the strange truth that Jesus might be heading for trouble that could lead to his untimely death. The more Peter thought about it, the more upset he became, until by the time the group arrived back home, he and his friends were "filled with grief" (Matthew 17:23).

Peter's attention was quickly diverted, however, when some tax collectors approached him. They were collecting a tax that had been established by Moses centuries before under the instruction of the Lord. For some reason, the tax collectors were unsure if Jesus had paid his taxes, and presumably they were unable or unwilling to ask Jesus. Ever the staunch supporter of his Master — except when he thought the Master was wrong — Peter insisted that Jesus always paid his taxes. But later Jesus, who seemed to know about the conversation held in his absence, asked Peter a rather ambiguous question about paying taxes. Did kings tax their own sons or other people? Peter answered that the kings taxed people other than their own families. Jesus replied that accordingly, sons must be exempt from paying taxes and implied that as his Father had instituted the tax — way back in Moses' time — He didn't need to pay it. This was no doubt a novel idea to Peter. *Hmm, I wonder if I'm exempt, too.* But any thoughts of possible immunity were immediately banished when Jesus made it clear that He had every intention of paying the tax, even though He did not need to. He would gladly pay, rather than cause offense. Peter was deflated. *I guess I'm paying my taxes.*

Jesus told Peter to go down to the lake, take a line and a hook, and he would catch a fish that would have a coin — a four drachma coin — in its mouth. This would pay the tax obligations of both of them. Sure enough, Peter caught the fish, opened its mouth, and there was the predicted coin. To this day tourists in Galilee are regularly served "St. Peter's fish"—a fish that reputedly carries its young or a pebble or bright coin in its mouth.

This very private, supernatural display was intended to have a profound impact on Peter. Here was Jesus, clearly master of all that He surveyed, humbly paying his taxes. Such humility in close proximity with such majesty could not fail to make an impression. Peter had just witnessed what happened when the disciples lost their humility and forgot the source of their power — they became powerless. Now Jesus was teaching Peter that while power corrupts, humility is the solution.

Peter and the other disciples were being given tremendous influence that would increase after Jesus' death. Jesus wanted to preempt a power struggle that He undoubtedly saw on the horizon of his discipleship-training schedule. He was showing by his humility that the true source of power is uncorrupted and incorruptible. If they remained humble and continuously attributed their power to the Lord and not themselves, they too would remain uncorrupted.

On the walk back to Capernaum, when Jesus was out of earshot, one of the disciples brought up the subject of power structures in the coming kingdom. Perhaps they were thinking, *Maybe Jesus is going to be removed from the picture. He says He'll be killed. He'll be raised again in the Resurrection (whatever that is) — but who will fill the vacuum his passing will create?* We don't know what started the discussion or which disciples were there, but we do have a general idea of what was on their minds: *Who is the greatest in the kingdom of heaven? Will it be me?*

We can imagine the kind of argument that ensued. Knowing Peter, there can be little doubt that he had the inside track. If he were present, he would have made his case in characteristically robust fashion. He was one of the first to meet Jesus; he was one of the first to respond to his call; he was one of the inner trio in whom Jesus confided and who had witnessed the Transfiguration; he was the first to proclaim that Jesus was Messiah; he was the only one who had received the special revelation from heaven; he was the only one who had walked on water; he was the one who was called the Rock and who had been promised a specific role in building the church; and he had received the keys to the kingdom. Who else had a claim even close to his? He was and would be the greatest. *End of discussion.*

But not as far as James and John were concerned. They, too, had aspirations to greatness. John may have met Jesus even before Peter did. He, too, could claim to be a member of the inner three who had seen the Transfiguration — as could his brother James — and James and John had also been given a special name by Jesus, even if it was not exactly a compliment but a recognition of their hot tempers (see Mark 3:17). Later, John would become known as the "disciple whom Jesus loved."

Andrew could have spoken up and pointed out that if it hadn't been for him, Peter would not even be in the picture. His voice would be quickly drowned out by the insistence of Judas that, as he had been entrusted with the finances of the movement, he was admirably suited for the role of leadership. This position would be treated with withering scorn by Simon the Zealot, whose background of strong involvement in causes showed great leadership capabilities. Matthew, the former tax man, had special contacts with the Romans, good business sense, and obvious management skills.

Thomas was known for his thoughtful and analytical approach to problems.

Who knows what went on as they trudged that dusty road? We don't know, but we can make some educated guesses because just like us, these men were desperately human.

On their arrival in Capernaum, Jesus gathered the men together and to their great embarrassment asked them, "What were you arguing about on the road?" No one wanted to speak up. Not even Peter. Given his usual role as self-appointed spokesperson, does his silence speak loudly? Could he possibly have been the instigator of the argument?

When nobody spoke up, Jesus revealed that He knew exactly what the topic had been. I imagine they must have been mortified. By now, the disciples should have learned that "He did not need man's testimony about man, for he knew what was in a man" (John 2:25). He called a child over to his side — some people think it may have been Peter's child because they were probably meeting in his house. Pointing to the child standing awed in the midst of such imposing men, Jesus told the disciples that if they wanted to be great in the kingdom, they'd better start learning lessons in humility. They needed to become like the child standing shyly in front of them. "Whoever humbles himself like this child is the greatest in the kingdom of heaven," He said with great emphasis. Then He added, "If anyone wants to be first, he must be the very last, and the servant of all."

These men seemed far from adopting the attitude of a child. Neither did being a servant fit into the aspirations of these men who were clearly more interested in posturing as powerbrokers.

Pressing home the point, Jesus took the child in his arms and showed how leaders in the kingdom were to embrace warmly even the most undistinguished person. Having been called by Christ to ministry, they needed to recognize that it is all too easy for the humble to be trodden underfoot, and they should be constantly on the lookout for "little ones" who could easily be damaged by the powerful. Jesus told a story about the kind of workers He was looking for. Such a person, if he had a hundred sheep, would not be so enamored of the big flock that he would lose sight of a single, lonely, straying sheep. On the contrary, he would go out of his way to devote time and energy to the needs of the lowly and the forgotten, the needy and the hurting of this world. In doing so, he would mirror the attitude of the Father in heaven, who is not willing that any "little ones should be lost" (Matthew 18:10-14).

Jesus was not finished. He went on to talk to his chastened men about handling conflict among those they were called to lead. Powerful people often manage disputes by eliminating those who disagree with them. A follower of Jesus, however, should approach the one who had wronged him — as a brother, not as an enemy — and try to talk through the issue. If the effort to resolve the difficulty doesn't work, another approach should be attempted, this time with witnesses. If that failed, then — and only then — stronger action could and should be taken. This approach is time-consuming and requires humility on the part of the person wronged, but that was exactly the point. If they were going to represent Christ, they had to be humble. Jesus told the disciples that if this approach worked and the two people reached a resolution, their efforts would be confirmed in heaven and their agreement would demonstrate that God had been at work (see Matthew 18:15-17).

When he had an opportunity, Peter took Jesus aside and asked, "Lord, how many times shall I forgive my brother when he sins against me?" He then suggested, with a great show of generosity, that perhaps he could extend his forgiveness "up to seven times." The rabbis in Peter's day said three times was sufficient, so Peter was pushing the limits big time. Perhaps he was trying to impress the Lord with his benevolence.

Jesus' reply was sharp and to the point. He said that seventy-seven times would be more appropriate, using an exaggeration to make the point, as He often did. Then He told Peter a simple story that packed a powerful punch line.

There was a king, one of whose subjects was deeply in his debt. On calling in the debt, the king found that the man could not pay, so he ordered the entire family to be placed in servitude. The debt was so huge that even if he and his family worked as slaves for the rest of their lives, they would not be able to repay it. So the king's debtor begged for his sovereign's mercy and was released.

As soon as he walked away from his obligations, he encountered a man who owed him a very small debt. Having been shown mercy, he might have been expected to tend toward leniency. But no. He brutally mistreated his debtor, insisting on repayment, and imprisoned the man. The king found out and promptly showed his displeasure by committing the unmerciful man to prison. Jesus explained, so that there could be no misunderstanding his point: The heavenly Father has forgiven his children so much that they, of all people, should be the most forgiving people (see Matthew 18:23-35).

Unfortunately, we all tend to hold grudges, make people pay, demand retribution rather than forgive. Our injured pride is mollified if we can exact some degree of payback. To forgive means our pride is left unsatisfied. It takes a humble person to accept wounded pride.

The lessons on leadership and humility were strong and unmistakable. Now the disciples had to work out how to be humble when they were clearly in positions of great potential significance. They were members of the Messiah's inner circle. Peter, James, and John were the inner, inner circle. Only Peter had the keys, and he was the Rock. Because of his prominence, his forceful personality, and his undoubted leadership qualities, Peter was most in need of humility. *This is not going to be easy.*

He was not aware of it, but there were more humbling experiences on the way. They would serve to teach him that if he amounted to anything, if he achieved anything of significance, it was directly attributable to Jesus. The Messiah had called him, perceived the potential in him, trained him, empowered him, and patiently put up with him. He owed everything to the Master — grounds enough for humility even in the most significant of men. He was learning, but the process was slow, and there were more painful lessons to come.

BRAVE ENOUGH TO THINK ABOUT IT

1. *Christ gives us opportunities to see that He's the Real Thing.* He took Peter, James, and John to the mountaintop to give them a glimpse of his full glory. He is more than just a great leader, a good example, or a great prophet. He is the Son of God. The Transfiguration was God's divine affirmation of the divinity of Christ.

   a. In what specific ways has God chosen to reveal his reality to you? Be concrete. Is it through your circumstances? Through Scripture? Through his voice speaking personally to you? Other ways?

   b. Because the Christian life is a life of faith, how do you find the balance between needing God to reveal himself to you and just believing? What helps you believe?

   c. If Christ is the Real Thing, what are some influences in your life that masquerade as real — real truth, real importance, real love — but are not? How do you resist their manipulation and stay focused on what's true?

2. *In our own strength, we're powerless; but if we rely on Christ's strength, nothing He wants us to do will be impossible.* The disciples, taking their new skills for granted, had fallen into the trap of thinking they were self-sufficient. They started believing that they themselves had what it takes to accomplish Christ's work, but found they were ineffective. Jesus taught them that some things can only be achieved through prayer. Praying ensures that we will have the right attitude of dependence, and that we will take the action of asking for help.

   a. In what areas of your life have you become so capable that you usually feel self-sufficient? How can self-sufficiency derail your success?

   b. Can you think of times when you've tried and tried to accomplish something that was seemingly an uphill battle, and it never occurred to you to ask for the Lord's help? What was the outcome? What could you have done differently? Could the result have been different?

   c. How do you apply Jesus' statement, "If you have faith as small as a mustard seed, you can say to this mountain, 'Move from here to there,' and it will move"? Can "mountains" really move? Is there evidence of this principle in your life?

3. *Because God has forgiven all of our sins, we need to forgive others.* Peter thought he was being generous in offering to forgive someone "up to seven times." But Jesus set him straight. He told Peter that unless he forgave his brother everything, God would not forgive him.

    a. Are you asking for forgiveness regularly? Are there any sins you don't think deserve forgiveness? Do you have a different standard for yourself than for others?

    b. Is there anyone in your life right now whom you are struggling to forgive? Or have no intention of forgiving? What can you do to change this?

    c. Do you think you should forgive people, even when they don't ask you for forgiveness? Why or why not?

4. *As we mature in Christ and find that He's using us in his work, it can become difficult to stay humble. But without humility, we have no place in God's kingdom.* Peter struggled with humility because of his prominence, his forceful personality, and his undoubted leadership qualities. But Jesus emphasized over and over the necessity of being a servant. We must remember that the only reason we are where we are is because Jesus calls us, trains us, and empowers us. When we realize that we owe everything to the Master and take no credit for ourselves, we experience true humility.

    a. How easy or difficult is it for you to accept the idea of humility? In what areas of your life is it especially challenging?

    b. Think about the leadership positions you've held or that you are now in. What circumstances have caused you to give in to your pride? In what ways have you become arrogant or misused your power? How can you keep from doing this in the future?

    c. What does humility look like in practice? How can you give God the credit for successes? What does it look like to be a "servant" in your work? In your family?

BRAVE ENOUGH FOR ACTION

I suspect that almost everyone has someone in their life who is difficult to forgive. Think about it. Against whom are you harboring a grudge? It might be someone who irritated you yesterday. It could be someone who seriously damaged you in your childhood. Who have you not forgiven?

I'm not going to tell you it's time to forgive him or her. But here's what I recommend. For the next week, pray for that person for a minimum of five minutes every day. Don't know what to pray? Stick to the basics. Pray for his or her peace, health, guidance, provision, blessing. Pray for all good things for him or her. Pray for God's will to be done in his or her life. And each day, pray that God will give you the desire and ability to forgive this person.

After a week, see if you can forgive that person. If you can, praise God. And be ready to forgive him or her again the next day if your grudge pops back up. If you find you're not yet ready to forgive, keep praying for the person, and keep praying for the strength to forgive. Don't stop until you're able to extend authentic forgiveness.

If you're carrying multiple grudges, how about repeating this process for each individual?

chapter 7

THE ROAD TO JERUSALEM

MATTHEW 19—20
MARK 10:1-45
LUKE 9:51—10:2

*F*or some time, Jesus had been indicating to his followers that rejection, suffering, and death awaited him in Jerusalem. The time had come for him to set out for the holy city, and his men went with him. They were unsure of his intentions and confused about his predictions and perhaps even troubled about his state of mind. But despite the obvious uncertainties, they stayed by his side.

Jesus, of course, had a great advantage over the Galileans. Luke tells us, "As the time approached for him to be taken up to heaven, Jesus resolutely set out for Jerusalem" (Luke 9:51). Putting this final stage of the journey in context, we realize that Jesus knew He was bound for glory — the glory that He had temporarily laid aside for the benefit of a lost humanity — and so was able to approach the impending horror of Jerusalem with firm resolve. His determination was born in the knowledge that He had come specifically for the purpose of dying and rising again. Although his sensitive spirit was repulsed by the thought of what would happen in his crucifixion, He set his jaw firmly and made his way to the inevitable suffering with redemption on his mind. Not his own, but the redemption of a world of sinners whose only hope was in his shed blood — a sacrifice for sin.

He had expressed a longing for heaven shortly after the Transfiguration, and the thought of being welcomed back there was undoubtedly in his mind. But none of this minimized the challenge facing him. There was only so much He could share with his disciples, lost as they were in their undeveloped understandings. So as He led the way along the hot and dusty roads, He knew the loneliness of leadership as no other leader has ever experienced it. But He continued purposefully toward his destiny.

The rising popularity of Jesus was clearly evident. While the religious leaders distrusted him, despised him, and looked for ways to discredit him, the masses revered him. They loved his miracles, which were often spectacular and greatly beneficial to those who felt his healing touch. It was no surprise, therefore, that as news of his journey toward Jerusalem spread, the people were waiting for him in large numbers. In fact, it appears that He intentionally sent a group of seventy people ahead to prepare the people for his arrival. He had lamented that the harvest was vast but there was a shortage of workers. But these few dozen, at least, were willing to go before him, preaching and healing and at times bearing rejection and ridicule.

Jesus was not welcome in all of the towns He passed through. The Samaritans weren't favorably disposed toward Jews, and in one particular town they went out of their way to be inhospitable to Jesus. James and John were furious. Brimming over with their apostolic authority, they suggested using their powers to bring down fire and judgment upon the villagers. The Master forcefully rebuked them.

This would not be the only instance in which the disciples would attempt to exploit their power. It's an unfortunate truth about humans — we tend to abuse the power we're given, particularly when we're not mature enough to handle it. Using our delegated authority is tricky business, requiring us to remain humble and not get heady with our influence. Power delegated from the Master is not for personal gain or for settling scores, but for advancing the concerns of the kingdom.

Interestingly, it appears Peter stayed out of this one, although I'm sure he had the opportunity to witness James and John's fury and their reprimand from Jesus. He probably even shared his friends' indignation at the insult to their Master. Could it be possible that, amidst his blunders, Peter's transformation was coming along in leaps and bounds? I picture him sitting it out, almost shaking his head at his old friends. *They should know better by now.*

Sometimes in the great crowds that gathered around Jesus, there were individuals who particularly captured his attention. One such man volunteered to join Jesus, but apparently he changed his mind hurriedly when he was given more details of the hardships of discipleship. Another man, when he was called, said he'd be glad to accompany Jesus provided he could first bury his father. He was told bluntly to get his priorities sorted out. A similar response was given to another man who simply asked for permission to bid his family farewell before heading out with Jesus.

We're not told how the disciples handled these apparently callous responses to what we would regard as perfectly reasonable requests. The demands of discipleship must have been heavy on their minds. As Jesus conveyed his high expectations of people, the wheels were turning in Peter's mind. *Why's He being so hard on them? He wasn't that tough with us.* He would have been forced to contemplate once again the difficulties in following this Master. *At least He doesn't hide anything from us.* There was no fine print in the call He extended. But the fact that the requirements were clearly stated didn't mean Peter understood them right away, any more than we do today.

It's possible that the man who wanted to bury his father and the other man who wanted to say goodbye to his family were trying to do what the Law commanded: "Honor your father and mother." Jesus had explained that He was not opposed to the Law. In fact, He had come to fulfill it. So He was neither undermining basic divine principles, nor was He diminishing the importance of family relationships. It seems that by his hard answers to their requests, He was explaining that even the most precious relationships on earth must take second place to a disciple's allegiance to the Master.

Our parents warrant our respect because they grant the gift of life, and they provide care and comfort. But Jesus offers the gift of eternal life, and He meets the deepest needs of our physical, emotional, and spiritual beings. Husbands, wives, children, and other family members deserve honor because of who they are and the role they play in our lives. But the honor due to the Creator, Redeemer, and Sustainer of our souls far transcends all other honors. Perhaps being a devoted follower of Christ could be considered one way to honor parents and families. Thinking about it, the disciples recognized the legitimacy of what Jesus was saying. It would be another matter to work out the "balance" between their responsibilities to the Lord and to their families. It's one of the biggest issues we still wrestle with today, requiring careful thought and godly insight.

As Jesus was leaving one of the villages, a wealthy young man of considerable social standing threw status and dignity to the wind, ran after Jesus, flung himself at his feet, and cried out, "Good teacher, what must I do to inherit eternal life?" Jesus, seeing into the heart of the young man, told him to keep the commandments. The young man promptly answered that he did — in fact, since boyhood he had been meticulous in this regard. But apparently he felt that he needed more than a religious code. He was looking for a fuller understanding of life eternal, and he was seeking some assurance that he might attain it.

There was something about the earnestness and sincerity of the man that touched Jesus' heart. He replied that there was only one thing missing in the young man's life, and it could quickly be remedied if he would sell his possessions, give the proceeds to the poor, and join Jesus' group. Then he would have what he lacked: treasure in heaven. This was more than the young man was prepared to do, even if it meant the difference between eternal life and eternal condemnation. Clearly, material considerations were gripping his heart and controlling his life. Despite his sincere belief that he was keeping the Law, he really did not love his neighbor enough to share with him, and he did not love God as much as he loved money. Jesus' astute observation of the man's heart had quickly identified his need for repentance and submission to Christ's lordship. A response that, sadly, he was unwilling to make.

How devastating to each of us when we see ourselves in this man. He was rich and unable to part with all he had accumulated. We may not think of ourselves as wealthy, but the reality is that if we have a home, a car, furniture, and food regularly on the table, we are wealthy compared to most of the world and indeed, most people throughout history. So it is not surprising that the idea of giving up our material possessions hits us where we live.

With great sadness, Jesus explained how hard it is for wealthy people to enter the kingdom. It is as difficult as trying to push a fully grown camel through the eye of a needle. After their initial amusement at Jesus' ridiculous illustration, the remark brought a quick response from the disciples, who had been brought up to believe that material wealth was the Lord's special blessing to deserving people. In our culture, one advantage we have over Peter and his friends is that we've been stripped of the notion that rich people "deserve" their wealth. Our newspapers are filled with stories of greedy, corrupt, and immoral individuals whose affluence is beyond the imagination of the average person. We see people whose careers are devoted to entertainment making millions, and others who have given up everything to help the poor and spread the Word of Christ having trouble keeping the lights on month to month. We have no illusions of material wealth being distributed on a merit basis.

But in the disciples' minds, the young man was financially blessed because he was most deserving, an obvious candidate for the kingdom and a certainty to inherit eternal life. How could Jesus possibly suggest otherwise? This was all very perplexing to people who had always worked on the assumption that actions have consequences, and good behavior guarantees blessings. So they asked despairingly, "Who then can be saved?" Jesus told them that gaining salvation by human effort was impossible, but not to worry, because "with God all things are possible" (Matthew 19:26). He was telling them that salvation is not by works, but by grace. It is not earned or deserved. It is freely granted as a gift. It is not given to the deserving — because there are none.

Peter, not liking what he was hearing, couldn't keep quiet. He protested, "We have left everything to follow you!" If salvation wasn't a reward for good behavior, what benefits could the disciples expect as a reward for the selfless abandonment of their lives to Jesus' cause? *Surely Jesus is not suggesting my sacrifice means nothing.*

Jesus assured Peter that his sacrifice, which was considerable, could not earn him eternal salvation but would not go unnoticed in heaven. The Father would make sure he was compensated for his life of service. Jesus even suggested the disciples would receive back a hundred times all they had given up, both before and after they entered heaven.

The teaching that came out of the incident was reinforced by one of Jesus' inimitable stories. A farmer had hired laborers early one morning, negotiated a wage with them, and set them to work. Later in the day, he hired more, and in the evening, still more. He paid all the workers the same amount at the end of the day. Understandably, the men who had worked the most objected that those who had worked less were being paid the same amount. The farmer pointed out that he had paid each man exactly what he had promised and, as it was his own money, he was free to be generous and it was none of their business.

Peter probably had some sympathy with the objecting workers. *Doesn't exactly seem fair.* But Jesus was illustrating how justice and grace work. Justice was done, in that the men who had worked all day got what they earned. Justice gives us what we deserve. But grace was extended when those who had done relatively little were given what they hadn't earned. Grace gives us what we don't deserve. In the divine economy, this is the way it works, and sinners should be grateful.

Still . . . doesn't seem fair. Even today, we have a hard time accepting these principles of justice and grace. We're all too willing to accept grace when it comes our way. But when it's extended to someone else who appears totally undeserving, well, that's another story. Is it fair for me to spend my entire life sacrificing for the cause of Christ, only to know that a mass murderer can experience a deathbed conversion and end up in heaven with me? Jesus wants us to acknowledge that we're all sinners, unworthy to judge each other's sin, and each of us is being extended truly amazing grace by being in the presence of Jesus.

There was another difficult incident during the journey to the holy city that gave the disciples more food for thought. Some of the Pharisees, who were becoming increasingly hostile to Jesus, had challenged him on the thorny subject of divorce. A great debate between followers of Rabbi Hillel and Rabbi Shammai was raging at that time. The argument was over what constituted valid grounds for divorce — if there were any. Hillel's followers were quite liberal on the issue; Shammai's, more conservative. The Pharisees probably hoped to get Jesus to come down on one side of the argument or the other, thus embroiling him in a diversionary controversy. But He was too smart for them.

In those days women had practically no rights and the men had all the power. If a man wanted to divorce his wife, he was free to do so "for any and every reason" (Matthew 19:3). Jesus indicated that in his opinion, while Moses had reluctantly conceded the possibility of divorce, the men did not have the freedom to divorce for any and every reason. Their "rights" in this regard had to be severely curtailed, and at the same time, women's rights were to be dramatically improved. This was strange teaching to the ears of the men, who complained, "If this is the situation between a husband and wife, it is better not to marry." A remark that, in our day, would raise the ire of many a woman, who need not be a feminist to be outraged at the selfishness of these men. In a few short words, Jesus had demolished the established concepts of male superiority and female inferiority. Red-blooded Galilean fishermen could hardly be expected to accept this teaching calmly.

But there was an even more troubling incident en route to Jerusalem. The mother of James and John approached the Lord, presumably with the full compliance of her sons, and asked for a special favor. All she wanted was for her sons to occupy the two most prestigious positions in the soon-to-be-established kingdom — one on the right side of Jesus, the other on his left. The blatant arrogance of this request, even after making allowances for the mother's ignorance of Jesus' recent teachings, was mind-boggling. The other disciples were outraged. Perhaps each of them was convinced he was the most likely candidate for the cherished position. I wonder if Peter, having learned some lessons by now, recognized the complete inappropriateness of any of them making this request.

Jesus turned down the request of the mother and sons, citing their lack of understanding of all that would be entailed in such positions of leadership. The brothers assured Jesus that they did understand and were fully capable of handling the situation. So the Master told them that He did not have the authority to grant such a request. Jesus had every right to be exasperated at their audacity, but instead He treated them kindly.

Knowing the other disciples were fuming, Jesus called them together and reminded them that their ideas of leadership were influenced by secular styles, meaning that people in power usually lorded it over everyone else and took advantage of their own authority. Jesus had never practiced such an approach, and neither should they. He didn't mention any names, but He stressed that those wishing to be great in the kingdom must be servants — certainly not a new teaching, but it had previously fallen on at least two pairs of deaf ears. Jesus concluded the intense teaching by reminding them that his mission was to serve, and He would do it by the ultimate act of service — giving his life as a ransom. This last statement was a new twist on what He had already said about his impending death, and once again, it's doubtful the disciples understood the significance of the words at the time. They certainly would get it after the events of the cross. In the meantime, they could only ponder what was said and try to grasp the implication.

Peter had more than enough to think about as he followed Jesus from town to town. The Master's healing touch in the lives of the multitudes was powerful and life-changing. His opponents were increasingly brazen in their antagonism. His teaching was more and more demanding. So Peter and his friends were required to do the difficult work of rethinking strongly held positions and deciding exactly where they stood. They had to think not only about their relationship to the Lord, but also whether they would accept and eventually spread his radical teaching. This, by the way, describes the life of the follower, even today. We must think about our relationship with the Lord, and decide what to do with his teachings.

Discipleship is all about following. But what if the follower discovers the leader is going in an unanticipated direction? Or what happens when the way becomes rough and the expected rewards are not forthcoming? Well — people tend to stop following. They take a break; they decide to go "so far and no further." Enough is enough. The development of heart and soul and the preparation for life and ministry grind to a halt.

In Peter's case, he was once again being challenged to think outside his box. It was no fault of his that he had been born a Jew, had lived all his life in Galilee, and had earned a living by fishing. He was, to a large extent, a product of his culture, a creature of his times. So are we. We have imbibed the thought patterns of our day; we have to a large extent adopted the mind-set of our environment.

But while time, culture, and events mold us, discipleship challenges the mold and makes us anew. It requires facing up to entrenched ideas, evaluating cherished ambitions, analyzing presuppositions, and relentlessly checking motives in the light of who Jesus is, what He said, where He's leading, and what He expects us to do.

Then there's the issue of disappointments along the way. Things don't work out as we expected they would when we met Jesus and joined his cause. His pace is faster than we thought, his expectations are more rigorous than imagined. The direction He takes leads to more trouble than we bargained for; his rewards don't always compensate for the bumps and bruises collected along the way. So what happens? Some head for the bushes and hide. Far too many fold their tents and steal away silently into the night. And others keep on keeping on. But how?

By learning to look at the blessings along the way that speak of grace available on a moment-by-moment basis. By looking backward to a cross and forward to a throne. By always keeping in mind the suffering Jesus — dying for me. By looking upward to the glory and seeing Jesus praying and waiting for me. By always remembering the risen Lord Jesus, whose Spirit He has sent to live in me.

There was a lot more to being Jesus' disciple than Peter had ever imagined. Many of his previously held and deeply cherished ideas were seriously challenged. But amidst his bewilderment and uncertainty, Peter kept on following. His Master had set out for Jerusalem, where it seemed untold horror possibly awaited, but Peter steadfastly followed. Puzzled and troubled, but loyal and brave. A good man despite his obvious flaws.

BRAVE ENOUGH TO THINK ABOUT IT

1. *Even the most precious relationships on earth are second in priority to our relationship with Christ.* This can be one of the most difficult lessons in discipleship. After all, why does God bless us with spouses and children if not for us to take care of them? But our task is to realize that while we have responsibilities to other people, our most important responsibility is to God.

   a. Read 1 Timothy 5:8. How can you reconcile this verse with Jesus' teaching that He takes priority?

   b. Do you think Jesus is asking people to neglect their families and responsibilities in order to follow him? If so, why would He do this? If not, then what is He saying? Give evidence for your answer.

   c. Are you adequately balancing kingdom demands with other commitments? How can you know whether you are or not? In our culture of busyness, is this balance even possible? How?

2. *While there is nothing evil about wealth in itself, being attached to the things money can buy makes it impossible to enter the kingdom.* Jesus doesn't ask every person to get rid of all their possessions in order to follow him. Certainly, this is the calling for some, but not all disciples of Christ. However, we each need to evaluate how strong a grip our material things have on our hearts. The stronger we are attached to our possessions, the more necessary it is to let them go in order to get our "heart priorities" straight and learn about really loving Jesus.

   a. Read 1 Timothy 6:10. Do you see yourself in this verse? Why or why not?

   b. How can you assess whether you love your stuff more than you love God? What are some of the signs? Why can't you love your stuff and love God, too? (See Matthew 6:24.)

   c. What would you do if you felt God calling you to simplify your lifestyle in order to focus better on him? Would you do it, and if so, how? If not, how would you justify your choice? How difficult would it be for you to simplify?

3. *Being a disciple requires us to let go of old ways of thinking and make clear decisions about where we stand with Christ and his teachings.* Peter was challenged by many of the things Jesus taught. He constantly had to reevaluate his perception of the truth. He had to decide if he would accept Jesus' words and if he would be willing to share these words with others.

   a. What "old ways of thinking" have you been challenged to relinquish since becoming a disciple of Christ?

   b. Which teachings of Jesus have you questioned the most? Which have been hardest to accept? Why?

   c. Which of Jesus' teachings do you, or would you, find easiest to share with others? Which would be the most difficult? Why?

4. *Jesus doesn't promise that following him will be an easy road.* Like Peter, we are in for some surprises when we commit to Christ. His expectations are rigorous. We meet with disappointments. The rewards don't always seem to compensate for the trouble. But by focusing on the blessings, the love, and the grace that flow from him, we gain the fortitude to keep following.

   a. When life's demands are hard, how does "looking backward to the cross and forward to the throne" make a difference?

   b. On the scale of easy to difficult, what did you think being a follower of Jesus would be like before you were one? How does that compare to reality?

   c. What gives you the fortitude to keep following Jesus even when it's hard?

BRAVE ENOUGH FOR ACTION

This might be a good time to make an assessment of your priorities. Take action on the question: Which do you love more, God or your stuff? Write down a list of all the things you do in daily life to acquire things, maintain things, and use things. What percentage of your time is spent on these activities? Now make a list of all the things you do to please God and nurture your relationship with him. Compare your lists. Do you think you need to make any changes?

If you'd like to take it a step further, sell a treasured possession and give the money to the poor. Pray about it first. Ask God what He would like you to give up. Ask him also to show you what to do with the money. Then follow through. See if you can do all of this without any expectation of reward in this life — do it just to store up treasure in heaven.

chapter 8

ECSTASY AND PERPLEXITY

MATTHEW 21–24
MARK 11–13
LUKE 19:28-44

*T*he road from Jericho to Jerusalem was narrow, hot, and steep. It wound precariously around steep cliffs next to deep canyons, climbing more than 3,000 feet before arriving at the summit of the Mount of Olives. From this vantage point, Peter and his companions had a magnificent panoramic view of the city, dominated by the temple that glistened in the unrelenting sunlight. As they arrived on Olive's summit, Peter looked down on the city. *What will happen here? What kind of reception will we get?* Jesus' popularity had soared with the common people but plummeted with the elites. It was possible they'd be greeted by rapturous crowds clamoring for another miracle. Then again, they might be met by the angry ruling priests. Would there be another verbal showdown between Jesus and his opponents?

The powerful elite had let it be known that they would arrest Jesus if they could lay their hands on him. The disciples had heard that these men wanted Jesus eliminated. Accordingly, while Jesus did not go into hiding, He had been careful to stay in remote areas where the authorities could not easily find him and He was surrounded by supportive local people. This way He was relatively safe, because the authorities wanted to avoid an uprising — something that would surely occur if they arrested Jesus in the presence of many followers.

But the city of Jerusalem was another story. There, it would be difficult to stay out of sight. Jesus would attract crowds wherever He went. Peter's trepidation grew.

As they approached one of the small villages dotting the Mount of Olives, Jesus turned to two of his men — probably Peter and John (see Luke 22:8) and gave them surprising instructions. They were to go into the village where they would find a female donkey and its young colt. They were to untie the animals and walk away with them. Should anyone ask what they were doing, they should simply reply, "The Lord needs them and will return them."

The two men were not in the habit of walking off with other people's donkeys, so they must have felt some unease as they made their way into the village with this peculiar assignment. But they had learned to do what they were told. In the early days when they went to the wedding in Cana and the wine had run out, Jesus had told them to do some very strange things with water that made no sense at all. But Mary, his mother, had quickly intervened, telling them, "Whatever he tells you to do, just do it." So they had done what He said and the rest, as they say, was history. Water became wine. It was the same when Jesus had told Peter to throw newly cleaned nets back into the water even though the fish were nowhere to be seen.

Peter had complied only because of the compelling voice in which Jesus had commanded him. Peter's haul was legendary. These men had learned that "theirs was not to reason why" where the Lord was concerned.

The owner of the donkeys asked the two men what they thought they were doing. The disciples replied as instructed, and the owner let them take the animals. Just like that. Jesus gave every indication that this was precisely what He'd expected, and He calmly sat on the colt and headed down the side of the mountain. They had climbed the long ascent from Jericho to Bethany, and He had shown no signs of fatigue. But now He wanted to ride on the short descent into the city. *It makes no sense.* Later they would realize He was being careful to fulfill Zechariah's ancient words, "See, your king comes to you, righteous and having salvation, gentle and riding on a donkey, on a colt, the foal of a donkey" (Zechariah 9:9).

As they came down the hillside, the crowds following him merged with even greater crowds who had rushed out of the city to meet him. Somebody started to recite verses from Psalm 118— "Hosannah to the Son of David, blessed is he who comes in the name of the Lord." The crowd took up the chant, cloaks were thrown beneath the colt's feet, and branches and twigs torn from nearby trees were strewn on the road.

Some Pharisees were in the crowd and could not tolerate the acclamation that was being heaped on Jesus. They shouted above the noise, "Tell your disciples to be quiet." Jesus, who was calm and cool despite all the clamor, replied, "I tell you, if they keep quiet, the stones will cry out." *The stones ... what?* Peter tried to imagine rocks shouting. He realized Jesus was saying that the praise being heaped upon him was good and right, and in fact, so appropriate that if the people stopped, nature herself would find it impossible to keep quiet. This was a triumphant moment. The King was entering his domain. He was arriving at the point in time for which He had temporarily vacated eternity. He had journeyed from heaven to this mideastern town on planet Earth to fulfill his destiny, and all nature was charged with the electricity of the event. This was Jesus' triumphal entry into Jerusalem.

But as Jesus looked out over the city, He wasn't celebrating. While the people shouted out his praises, his eyes filled with tears for Jerusalem. Peter and his friends were perplexed. Their spirits were sky high, but the Master was in tears. The people of Jerusalem were welcoming them with open arms. The city lay at his feet. But He was despondent.

"If you, even you, had only known on this day what would bring you peace — but now it is hidden from your eyes," He said (Luke 19:42). Their Prince of Peace had arrived, and they were totally missing the point. They loved his miracles and approved of his supernatural power — and they still envisioned him as their new king. They didn't realize that this was God's personal visit to them, that this was God appearing in the flesh and preparing their salvation for all eternity. They didn't know this would be their last chance to hear and understand what He was trying to teach. All they saw was an enigmatic man, riding on a donkey.

Jesus knew many in the crowd would turn against him in a matter of hours, and in a few short years Jerusalem would suffer at the hands of marauding armies and be reduced to rubble. He told them they were going to be decimated by enemies. The children were waving palms and crying "Hosannah," and Jesus was saying that they'd all soon be murdered. Jesus was predicting that the streets now littered with branches would soon be strewn with rubble torn from stately buildings by hateful hands.

Peter loved Jesus, revered him, and followed him with his whole heart. But he still did not understand his Master. He was continually being confronted with fresh challenges, insights, and lessons. As they arrived in the Jerusalem area for the last time, it seemed to Peter that a number of things frankly didn't make a lot of sense. There was Jesus telling them to help themselves to a man's donkey. There was Jesus weeping at what appeared to be his moment of triumph. There was Jesus predicting destruction and gloom on this, his glorious day. He seemed to operate in a different world from theirs. Once again, Peter grew frustrated. *Will I never understand him?*

Modern followers of Jesus have the same problem. We are trained to think clearly and rationally, and we're expected to make sound decisions. But at times, Jesus tells us to do things that go against the grain. They are embarrassing, they are humiliating, they appear to be counterproductive. They can be risky. Sometimes they make no sense at all.

Naturally we need to exercise great care in embarking on ventures that don't make sense. We need to make sure that we are acting in obedience to a substantive word from the Lord. We don't do things that don't make sense just to prove something to ourselves or others. We must try to discern the divine will, and do it.

On arriving at the temple, Jesus astonished Peter by repeating an action that had proved highly controversial in the early days of his ministry. Temple worshipers were required to pay a half-shekel tax in temple currency. As a service to those who came from a distance and whose currency was either Greek or Roman, provision was made for them to exchange their currency in the temple precincts. But this service had been grossly abused, and extortion was the rule of the day. Jesus would not tolerate it. So, as He had done two or three years earlier, He threw over the tables of the moneychangers and with a remarkable display of intensity and strength, He threw them out. Physically. As He was doing this He shouted, "This is supposed to be a house of prayer and you've made it a den of robbers." Some of the people who heard this recognized immediately that He was quoting Jeremiah, who in his day had spoken out about the way people took great pride in temple ritual but had little interest in spiritual reality.

That night, Jesus went out of Jerusalem and spent the night in Bethany. The next morning on his return to the city, Jesus was hungry. He headed toward a fig tree covered with leaves. Although it was not the season for fruit, the presence of leaves suggested there might be some, but closer inspection showed there was nothing but leaves. To the astonishment of the disciples Jesus said clearly, "May you never bear fruit again." The Master's rare display of frustration and irritation directed at the tree raised a few eyebrows. *What's gotten into him?* But He had been under great stress, so maybe it was understandable. Later on, Peter noticed that the tree had completely withered at Jesus' words, and on pointing this out to Jesus, he was told in effect, "With the right kind of faith it is possible to do more than wither a tree. You can remove mountains and demolish obstacles."

Eventually the disciples put the two events together — the cleansing of the temple and the cursing of the fig tree — and understood the lesson. The people Jesus evicted from the temple were like the fig tree in that they looked as if they were doing something spectacular, but they were in reality producing nothing in terms of fruit (the leaves looked nice, but you couldn't eat them). Jesus would not tolerate it, and in each case, He clearly showed his abhorrence.

Huge crowds were filling the city. Jesus' popularity was at an all-time high, and it seemed the more popular He became, the more outspoken He got. The chief priests were facing a massive dilemma. He had to be silenced or they ran the risk of a popular uprising. But how could they silence him? Any action in that direction could provide the spark that would ignite a riot they could not control.

Knowing they could not win by using force, they resorted to trickery. They tried to get him to make a public statement that would open him up to a charge of sedition and place him in danger of arrest by the Romans. "Is it right to pay taxes to Caesar or not?" they asked, in a show of genuine respect for his wisdom. Their thinking was pathetically transparent. If He said "Yes, of course, you should pay taxes to Caesar," the crowds who detested the taxation would be incensed and hopefully his popularity would soon dissipate. But if He said, "No, you shouldn't pay him a dime," the Romans would be there in a flash. They had him, they thought.

Jesus' reply was masterful. Borrowing a coin, He showed it to them, and got them to admit that it bore Caesar's image and an inscription attributing deity to Caesar. Then He said, "Give to Caesar what it rightfully his, and to God what is rightly his." They were flummoxed, and turned and left. At first glance, it appears that He had simply won a debating point and embarrassed his opponents. But in fact, He had succinctly outlined a principle that is relevant for his servants to this day. Our dual citizenship — in the world and in God's kingdom — requires that we pay money to those we owe for the benefits we receive, but we owe our primary obedience and commitment to God.

To the satisfaction of the crowds, He started to tell the chief priests and elders some of his patented stories. Each one seemed to make a similar powerful point. There was a parable about two sons, one of whom said he would work for his father but didn't, and the other who said he wouldn't work, but did. Jesus pointed out that there are some people who say they'll serve the Lord but don't, and others who said they won't honor the Lord but have a change of heart.

Then there was the story of the landowner who planted a beautiful vineyard, leased it to some local tenants, and at harvest time sent his servants to oversee the gathering of the fruit. But the locals stoned and killed the servants, and when the landowner sent his son, they killed him, too. Jesus asked, "What do you think the landowner would do?" The people replied, "He would punish the tenants and get some new ones who will give him the fruit at harvest time."

Slowly it dawned on Jesus' opponents, the religious leaders, that He was talking about them. They were the ones who in Jesus' view had said they would serve the Lord and did not, while the "undesirable" people He associated with had come to repentance and were living a life of blessing. These authorities were the ones to whom the Lord had given great provision and blessing, but they had spurned his grace and were plotting violence against the Father's Son. Jesus told them that the kingdom of God was about to be taken away from them and given to people who would produce fruit. (Hearkening back to the fig tree, whose ability to produce fruit was taken away after it had failed to do so.)

Each in turn, the Sadducees and then the Pharisees came at Jesus with their questions designed to trip him up. They were using every bit of brainpower they had to get him to say something that would warrant arrest. But it was his game, and they couldn't win. Peter looked on, admiring. *He's unbelievable.* It was like watching a competition in which the reigning champion repeatedly rebuffed his opponents' attempts to topple him. The crowds were thoroughly enjoying watching the Master at work, but Jesus didn't appear to be enjoying his verbal victories. Quite the opposite, his demeanor was serious.

In fact, He began a long speech denouncing the rampant hypocrisy of the religious leaders of the nation. His choice of language was the harshest Peter had ever heard him use. He called the

Pharisees hypocrites, blind fools, sons of hell, snakes, and a brood of vipers. He accused them of being so committed to legalistic niceties while ignoring massive spiritual principles, that they were like men who gag on a gnat but swallow a camel. That probably got an appreciative laugh from the crowd, but Jesus was not joking. He told the people they might have to obey the laws the Pharisees set for them, but they were not to "do what they do," because the Pharisees didn't practice what they preached. He said the Pharisees worked hard to "shut up the kingdom of heaven" for other people, yet they themselves would never enter (Matthew 23).

Strong stuff. This is the kind of Sunday sermon that tends to send the congregants packing, never to return. When people are hit between the eyes with the truth, their first response is often to run. But there was not a trace of vindictiveness in Jesus' strong words. As a surgeon's scalpel cuts deep and severs diseased tissue out of compassionate concern, so Jesus' cutting remarks were uttered from a grieving and broken heart. "O Jerusalem, Jerusalem," He called out in anguish, "how often I wanted to gather you like a hen gathers chickens, but you would not come to me." He went on to once again predict the desolation of their city, and to tell them that their chance to acknowledge him had passed, as they would not see him again until his triumphant return at the end of the age. With that, He rose and made his way quietly through the crowd, leaving behind an assembly of the elite beside themselves with rage.

As the disciples followed Jesus away from the crowds, they paused and looked back at the temple, standing massive and magnificent in the evening light. "Stunning," one of them remarked, strangely moved by the sight. "Yes," said Jesus, "and it'll soon be totally demolished." The knowledge was devastating to the disciples. They trudged in heavy silence up the slopes of the Mount of Olives one more time. Close to the summit, Peter, James, John, and Andrew drew the Lord to the side and said to him, "Tell us more. When will this happen? Does this mean we're coming to the end you've been predicting? Will there be a connection between this awful event, and the return you just told us about in the temple?" At last, Jesus seemed to have their attention. Finally, they seemed to be hearing him.

Jesus sat down on the mountain. Gathering the group around him, He began patiently to outline the things they needed to know about the future. The disciples had heard Jesus mention "the end of the age," but their understanding of this ominous phrase was limited. They recognized that it might have something to do with a final assessment and verdict on all of humanity. Now that Jesus had predicted the destruction of the temple, they put two and two together and assumed that when the temple was demolished, human existence would cease. But Jesus had not said that. He outlined a series of events before "the end" that would be characterized by betrayals, violence, and persecution. Many would pose as messiahs and lead people astray. International strife would break into war, spiritual life would deteriorate, and natural disasters would add to human misery. But this difficult period would also offer opportunities for "the gospel of the kingdom" to be preached "to all nations." In the midst of darkness there would be a bright and shining light — the good news that God had not deserted his people and had visited the planet to redeem them.

He told them that the present generation would not pass away before the temple was destroyed. But the "end of the age" would come at a different time. He assured them that "the Son of Man" would return, and his description of that moment left no doubts in their minds that it would be a glorious and powerful event, spelling out great sorrow for those who had rejected him and unspeakable joy for those who had longed for his coming.

Jesus warned that the signs of the end of the age would be difficult to ascertain. There would be abundant evidence over an extended period that would point relentlessly to the inevitability of a final day of reckoning by God. But because no specific date was available, the followers of Jesus must live constantly on the alert, as if any day might be their final day on earth.

It was a somber and thoughtful Peter who made his way over the crest of the mountain to Bethany that night. He would never forget seeing Jesus weeping over Jerusalem while the people were dancing in the streets. Incredibly, Jesus had not stopped them — in fact, He had defended their actions. The Master knew the people needed the freedom to celebrate. Praise and worship are an integral part of human existence. But they are not everything. Jesus was all too aware of the condition of the lost, the certainty of impending judgment, the shortage of time, the lack of workers, the immensity of the harvest, the pressing needs of the underprivileged — a heaven to be gained, a hell to be shunned.

Peter thought about the issues among God's people that needed to be addressed. Religious activity that was devoid of spiritual content. Spiritual profession that was without genuine fruit. Challenges concerning priorities — what belongs to Caesar and what belongs to God? Believers squabbling over insignificant fine points and ignoring glaring inconsistencies. Peter began to feel the burden of these issues.

He had long since realized that when he agreed to follow Jesus, he had no idea what he was getting into. Now, he had even less grasp of how it would all work out. But his confidence in the Master was unshaken, and he was still following.

BRAVE ENOUGH TO THINK ABOUT IT

1. *Each of us has both social and spiritual responsibilities, as illustrated by Jesus in his statement, "Give to Caesar what is Caesar's, and to God what is God's."* This is similar to the earlier teachings on balancing responsibilities to family and Christ. God created a world for us — and He expects us to live wisely and well in the world.

   a. What kinds of things in your life can be described as belonging to either "Caesar" or "God"? How can you tell the difference? How do you know what goes where?

   b. Because God clearly wants us to live "in the world," what does it mean when the Lord says we are not to be "of the world"? How can you accomplish being "in" but not "of"?

   c. In what ways do your social and spiritual responsibilities compete?

2. *It is easy to get caught up in the insignificant concerns of life while intentionally ignoring the things that matter.* Jesus accused the scribes and Pharisees of straining out a gnat but swallowing a camel. They spent all their time worrying about minor infractions of the law, and no time on the basics of justice and mercy and faith. They did things for show so they'd look good to others.

   a. What evidence of inconsistency is there in your life — that is, areas where your outward actions don't match your heart? Why is there this disconnect? How can you start working to change it?

   b. Jesus accused the scribes and Pharisees of cleaning the outside of the cup, while inside greed and self-indulgence remained. He told them to first clean the inside of the cup, then the outside would be clean (see Matthew 23:25). What did Jesus mean? How can you apply it to your life?

   c. Why is it so tempting to whitewash the outside of yourself to look good to others, while ignoring the sinful attitudes inside? Which is easier, to look good to others or to look good to God?

3. *Jesus doesn't tolerate people who claim to serve the Lord, but really don't, preferring instead to "look good" and serve themselves.* There is no place for these people in the kingdom. In the space of a couple days, Jesus cleared the temple of moneychangers and put a curse on a fig tree that was lush but fruitless. In both instances, He was demonstrating how abhorrent it is to him when someone acts like they love him and serve him, but don't. To profess faith without really having it is the ultimate insult to him.

   a. How much is your profession of faith backed up by your actions? What, specifically, do you "do" that professes your faith?

   b. In what ways is your life bearing fruit? How can your life, as well as your words, be a witness to Jesus?

   c. Religious activity can start out sincere but become corrupted, or lose its authenticity. Is there any evidence of this in your life? How does it happen? How can it be changed?

4. *Our joy in the Lord must be tinged with a serious grasp of the hour in which we live.* Just when it appeared Jesus was approaching his most triumphant moment, He became solemn and began predicting destruction and the end of the age. He warned the disciples that they needed to be ready at any moment because they wouldn't know when the Son of Man would return. He fervently stressed that they be watchful, always making sure their hearts were right, because no one would know precisely when the end would come.

   a. In what ways does Jesus want you to be ready for his return? How do you make sure your heart is right?

   b. If Jesus were to return today, would you be ready for him? Why or why not? What might you do to make sure you're ready?

   c. How does this teaching compare with Solomon's advice to hold on to joyfulness in life, to "eat and drink and be glad" (Ecclesiastes 8:15)? How can you be joyful yet mindful of the "urgency of the hour"?

BRAVE ENOUGH FOR ACTION

Whether or not we're ready for the return of Christ is a big question. Spend some time thinking about the condition of your life. Make two lists — your attitudes and your actions — and determine which things on these lists signify readiness and which signal your need for change.

If you see a need for change, ask God for forgiveness, and pray that He will show you what He wants you to do. Put together a plan of action to begin making these changes. Then get started.

In the process, don't forget about God's incredible grace and unbelievable mercy. Remember that He is looking at your heart.

chapter 9

An Unbelievable Day

MATTHEW 26:17-56
MARK 14—15
LUKE 22
JOHN 13—18

$\mathscr{P}$eter felt something in the air when he woke early on the first day of the Feast of Unleavened Bread. He had no idea of the stupendous events that would overtake him in the coming hours. He was deeply troubled by the animosity shown to Jesus by the authorities, coupled with the serious words that Jesus had spoken about the end of the age. It was a beautiful morning; the sun was rising brilliantly over Bethany, but clouds of foreboding were gathering over Peter's soul.

He thought about the many things that had to be done before they could celebrate the Passover. They had to travel to the city again, because the Passover meal had to be eaten within the walls of Jerusalem. They needed to rent a room; purchase unleavened bread, herbs, wine, and sauce; and procure a yearling lamb and take it to the temple to be sacrificed. All before sunset.

But the Master seemed to be in no hurry, so a delegation of disciples went to him and asked where they should start making preparations. To their surprise, He conveyed to Peter and John that everything was under control. It appeared He had made arrangements for a room where they could celebrate the Feast. So He told them to go to the city and they would see an unusual sight — a man carrying a water pot. The man would show them the room that was furnished and ready for them.

Peter and John pushed their way through the crowded narrow streets, purchased their goods, found the man with the water pot, inspected the room, and then joined the rest of the disciples and Jesus in the temple courts. Crowds of people were hurrying into the courts holding terrified bleating lambs that they handed to the priests to be sacrificed. Thousands of them. The animals' throats were slit; their blood was then passed from hand to hand in brimming bowls to be spilled at the base of the altar. Even the most hardened heart of the most experienced priest could not help being touched by the pitiful plight of the helpless, innocent lambs being slain for the sins of the people. Little did they know.

After the sacrifice, the men climbed the steps to the appointed room and noted that everything was in place for their Passover. With one exception. Under normal circumstances, there would have been a menial servant or slave responsible for removing the sandals of the guests and washing their feet. But no such person was in attendance. This immediately became a point of contention for the disciples. "I'm not going to do it." "Well, don't look at me." "If you think I'm going to wash your feet, you're crazy." Washing feet was the responsibility of people inferior to them. An argument ensued, showing that the old issue of "who was the greatest" was far from being resolved. Jesus quickly stepped in and reminded his fractious followers that He expected their attitude to be different. They were supposed to be learning from his example, and He personally had not come to be served, but to serve. Once again, He reminded them that greatness is not about power, but about grace and service.

Jesus went on to tell them they ought to be able to see the fingerprints of Satan in the way they were behaving. The enemy of their souls was trying to separate them from each other, to divide the group and hopefully conquer Jesus and his plans. Satan had discovered that Jesus was more than a match for him, but his disciples were vulnerable. Perhaps he could stop Jesus' movement if he could separate his followers and divert their energies to infighting rather than to Jesus' cause and the gospel.

Jesus turned to Peter and said pointedly, "But I've prayed for you Simon, that your faith may not utterly fail." Apparently, Peter was largely responsible for the acrimonious debate over greatness. Peter had let it be known that there was no way he, in his superior position, was going to do the job of a servant. *But what does that have to do with my faith? My faith won't fail!*

This was not turning out to be a good day for Peter. How could the Master imply in front of everybody that his faith was suspect? He, who had walked on water. He, who had first recognized the Messiah. He, who had consistently and vigorously led the way when the other disciples were lagging behind.

He was not a happy follower as he took his place, reclined at the table, and started to eat. Nobody's feet had yet been washed. An uneasy silence filled the room. The disciples were embarrassed; Jesus was deeply troubled. Then quietly, without warning, He uttered the stunning words, "One of you is going to betray me."

The disciples were incredulous. Someone spoke up, "Surely not, Lord." But Jesus insisted that the culprit was even at that moment in the room breaking bread with them. This was too much for Peter. *It can't be true. Who would it be?* Jesus went on to declare in somber words that the thing this man was about to do was so heinous that it would be better for him if he had never been born. But He added that while this man was entirely culpable for his dreadful action, what was happening was part of a great plan that had been hinted at in the ancient Scriptures.

The disciples were so unnerved by Jesus' words that they began to doubt themselves. "Surely not I," they said, until finally Judas, feigning horror and confusion, added his voice to the chorus. Jesus looked pointedly at him, saying, "You said it." With that, Jesus dismissed Judas, who went out into the dark night. Peter couldn't believe that one of their circle would betray the Master. Certainly not Judas, the treasurer. *If you can't trust the man with the money, who can you trust?* They all assumed he was going on a prearranged errand. In a macabre way, he was.

Jesus then got up from the table, discarded his outer garment, and wrapped a towel around his waist. Taking a bowl of water, He knelt and began to wash his disciples' feet. They were stunned into silence. Jesus made his way around the room, cleaning the feet of each self-conscious man. They listened to the water dripping into the bowl as He wrung the cloth, averted their eyes as He dried each foot with the towel, and nervously cleared their throats as the air grew thick with tension.

Wouldn't it have been nice if one of the disciples had volunteered to wash the others' feet? Clearly it was the custom to have your feet cleaned before sitting down to dinner. When no servant appeared, couldn't one of the men have relented? He could have grabbed the bowl of water and said with a sense of humor, "Alright, whoever wants clean feet, line up. It's now or never." But not one of them gave in. Washing feet was the ultimate in humility, and none of them was there yet.

Jesus made his way around to Peter, who leaped up and declared, "You shall never wash my feet." Jesus told Peter that he did not understand the significance of the foot washing, but it would become clear at a later date. In fact, if he wasn't washed, he couldn't be a follower of Jesus. This was all very confusing but one thing was clear — Peter had no intention of being left out of the group. So, with his characteristic enthusiasm, he exclaimed, "Fine then — give me a total bath!" The Master responded that he was not to worry, that with the exception of the one who had left the room, they were all clean.

The immediate lesson was a reiteration of that which Jesus had been teaching for months — to be a leader, a person must be a servant. But after the events of the next few hours, it became clear to them that, as Jesus washed dust from dirty feet with water, through his death He would cleanse souls from sin by his blood.

The assurance that Jesus had given Peter about being clean was encouraging, but the disciples were challenged by the lesson on humility. In washing their feet, He had given them an example, and their role in life was to follow that example meticulously. This was yet another pointed criticism on their arrogant attitudes and an unmistakable model of the leadership style that his followers were to adopt. He also made it very clear that this was not an optional style of leadership. It was the way they were to operate if they were to know the blessing of the Lord on their future. There would be a definite connection between blessing on their lives and a servant attitude in their hearts.

The Passover meal was turning out to be a difficult time, but Jesus followed the details of the traditional meal. Consequently, the disciples were startled when Jesus broke from the customary liturgy. Holding a piece of bread in his hand, He said, "Take and eat; this is my body." A little later when they drank the usual third cup of wine, he added similarly, "This is my blood of the covenant, which is poured out for many for the forgiveness of sins." There could be no doubt that He was investing the Passover feast with totally unheard-of significance, rooted in himself and in some way related to the shedding of his blood and the breaking of his body.

The disciples had little chance to ponder these alarming disclosures before Jesus made another shattering statement. "This very night, you will all fall away on account of me." Then as if to reinforce the impact of his words, He quoted the prophet Zechariah, "Strike the shepherd, and the sheep will be scattered" (Zechariah 13:7).

Peter had listened long enough. He didn't care what the prophet had said, and he didn't appreciate what the Lord was saying. *Zechariah was wrong back then, and Jesus is wrong now.* Admittedly, the opposition to Jesus was building, his life was being threatened and plots were being hatched to kill him. Maybe Jesus did think his body was going to be broken and his blood shed, whatever that meant, and perhaps He saw that as similar to a shepherd being struck down. But to suggest that he, Peter, was a sheep and would be so easily "scattered" was too much. He objected, "Even if all fall away on account of you, I never will." The Master's eyes pierced Peter's as He uttered, "This very night, before the rooster crows, you will disown me three times."

But Peter denied it. "I will never disown you." The other disciples, finally finding their voices, echoed his words.

This had to have been one of Peter's worst days ever. He had been singled out twice by the Master, once as a target for Satan and once as an imminent deserter. He had been embarrassed and humiliated. He had been mortified at Jesus cleaning his feet. Now he was being told he would disown Jesus — the man he'd been following faithfully for nearly three years! The One for whom he'd given up everything! It was unbelievable.

What could he do at this point? He might have wanted to get angry and storm off. He could've argued and pointed fingers. He could have walked quietly out of the room, never to return. Or he could have taken everything to heart and tried to think it through.

Or trusted that the Master was still on his side and decided he'd come this far, he might as well keep going.

It appears Peter made the latter choice, because at the conclusion of the meal, Peter was still there. Bravo, Peter. Courageously continuing to follow after all he'd been through.

While still at the Passover table, Jesus led the group in prayer. They had often been with him as He talked to the Father, but they had never heard him pray as He did that night. He asked the Father to glorify him so that the Father would be glorified through his actions. Then He prayed for the disciples. He talked about them being left in the world after He departed, and He asked that they would be safe as they went out into a hostile environment. Then He talked mysteriously about the people who would believe as a result of the ministry of these men. The disciples had little understanding of their future ministry, and they were not inclined to engage in ministry without the Master. Eventually they would understand what it was all about. But not at this moment (see John 17).

After prayer, He announced it was time to leave, and He told them they were going to a secluded olive garden called Gethsemane. The hour was late and the day had been long, but Jesus had often found rest and refreshment in this quiet place. On the way, He talked to them about his imminent departure. Peter insisted that he wanted to go with the Master, only to be told that it was impossible, but that he would follow later. Jesus also reassured his men that He would come back for them. But they didn't understand why they couldn't just go with him now, so that He wouldn't have to come back for them.

Jesus also talked about the Holy Spirit who would be sent to them during his absence. He tried to impress upon the disciples that the presence of the Holy Spirit in their lives would definitely be advantageous for them. But they couldn't see it. This talk of Jesus' departure made them very uncomfortable. A mysterious Holy Spirit was of little or no interest to them. They wanted to know where He was going. And why? And why couldn't they go with him?

On arrival at the garden, Jesus told his men that they were going to pray. As was often the case in special circumstances, Jesus took Peter, James, and John with him, and told them that his soul was overwhelmed with sorrow. He needed them to keep watch and to pray earnestly for him. Jesus went a little farther into the garden. There He prayed with great anguish to the Father about his imminent confrontation with sin and death and evil and the Devil himself, and most of all the unspeakable horror of being separated from the heart of the Father. He begged the Father to remove this upcoming horror from him — but promised the Father that He would do whatever the Father wanted.

Jesus returned to his disciples and found them not watching and praying, but sleeping. He woke them and said to Peter, "Could you not watch with me for one hour?" But Jesus did not upbraid them, despite his personal disappointment and his deep concern for these men who were in more danger than they realized.

Jesus went back to pray again. But as He returned to prayer, they went back to sleep. When He came and found them in repose, He left them alone. It was too late now. His enemies were on their way.

He decided the disciples might as well enjoy a few more minutes of blissful ignorance before facing the horrors of the night.

He returned to pray a third time. When He had finished, He roused his men. Pointing to the lights of a procession coming from the city, He told them his betrayer was about to arrive. It was time to go and face the momentous events for which He had come into the world.

Reluctantly they followed him with a deep sense of foreboding. There was a quiet solemnity about Jesus that was almost frightening. He was strangely calm but intensely focused. And there was something ominous about the approaching crowd with their blazing torches.

A detachment of the temple guard and Jewish officials surrounded them, conspicuously armed with swords and clubs. To the disciples' amazement, Judas stepped forward. In a prearranged signal, he embraced Jesus and kissed him. The kiss of a traitor — the ultimate act of hypocrisy. Jesus, fully aware of what Judas was doing, responded, "Friend, do what you came for." Friend! Amazing grace. The armed men leaped forward, grabbed Jesus, tied his hands, and started to lead him away. But they had failed to reckon with one man. Simon Peter.

Jesus had told his disciples that the time would come when they would be called to minister in difficult circumstances, and they would need to take the necessary steps to protect themselves, which included carrying swords. Now, as the servant of the high priest — a man called Malchus — stepped forward to oversee the arrest, one of these swords suddenly appeared in the fist of Peter. With a great swinging arc, he brought the sword crashing down on Malchus' head. At the last second, Malchus ducked. Peter's blow, which undoubtedly was intended to split the man from top to bottom, caught only Malchus' ear.

In the stunned silence that followed Peter's single-handed defense, a voice rang out. "No more of this!" Jesus was addressing both Peter and the armed soldiers. He told them they didn't need to come at him with swords and clubs. They saw him teaching daily in the temple — they could have arrested him there. He had made no attempt to evade them, and He wasn't interested in a fight. If He intended to use force, He would have called on ten thousand angels to come to his aid. But He had not called for them, because the events that were taking place were all part of a great cosmic plan of which they were ignorant. Then, to Peter's embarrassment, Jesus touched Malchus' bleeding head and healed the remnants of his ear. Turning to his captors, He said calmly and distinctly, "Darkness reigns." And to prove it, they led him away into the night, and the disciples ran for their lives. Including Peter.

He ran blindly, stumbling over half-buried roots. Forcing his way through trees and undergrowth, the branches slashed his face and tore at his robes. He had no idea where he was going. All he knew was that he had to get away. He must put as much distance as possible between the men holding Jesus and himself. Fear held his soul in a fierce grip. His lungs ached, tears stung his eyes, and his heart was breaking. He was on the run, driven by the fear of death.

Then in the darkness he heard someone else running, scrambling toward him. He crouched down and was able to see dimly the outline of the young man who stopped within a couple yards of him. Gasping for breath, the shadowy figure leaned against a tree. It was John. The two men saw each other and clumsily clung together, bonded by their common fear.

"What are we going to do?" John whispered.

"What can we do?" Peter replied.

"It's not right that we should run away."

"But what good will it do if we stay with Jesus? They'll arrest us, too."

"Let's follow and see where they're taking him and what they're going to do. Just don't let them see us," John suggested, and Peter agreed.

In the distance they could see the torches of the mob leading Jesus back into the city. They hurried after Jesus and his captors, but took care to maintain a discreet distance.

Eventually, the men leading Jesus arrived at the High Priest's palace. They arranged a meeting with Annas, a highly regarded elder statesman and former High Priest, who agreed to meet them in the courtyard. Meanwhile, John and Peter had been let into the courtyard as well, as John was known there. Annas began to interrogate Jesus. While he was talking, a young girl approached Peter and, thinking that she recognized him, said, "Aren't you one of this man's disciples?" Peter brusquely denied it and turned away from her. There was a charcoal fire that gave limited relief from the cold night air, and Peter sidled as close as he dared toward the group of servants gathered around it.

Annas, in an attempt to find out what charges could be leveled at Jesus, was questioning him about his teaching. But Jesus pointed out that there is no point asking a teacher what he has taught. Far better to ask the pupils. If they don't know what they've learned, they clearly haven't been taught. So He said, "Why question me? Ask those who heard me. Surely they know what I said." By this time, Jesus was aware that Peter stood in the shadows. While we can't say if He was intentionally giving Peter a chance to stand up and testify to the truth, the opportunity was undoubtedly there.

Peter rarely missed a chance to express an opinion. Given this critical opportunity to speak up, it would have been no surprise if he had boldly stepped forward to give a statement of his experience with Jesus. But he didn't say a word.

Jesus' response to Annas' question was perfectly reasonable. Nevertheless, an official stepped forward and struck Jesus across the face, rebuking him for answering the High Priest in such a way. Jesus calmly responded that the man should either prove Jesus' words untrue or explain why he hit someone for telling the truth. The calm courage of Jesus contrasted starkly with the silent cowardice of his formerly outspoken disciple.

At that point, another servant questioned Peter about his allegiance to Jesus, but this time Peter vehemently denied any such relationship. "I don't know the man." But he was not to be allowed to hide in the shadows. Another official came to him and said, "Didn't

I see you with him in the olive grove?" Peter cracked and shouted, "God strike me dead if I was with this man in the olive grove." Such is the language of a desperate man, compounding denial with oaths and curses.

At that moment a cock crowed and the sound of its strident call reverberated around the courtyard. Jesus heard. Peter heard. Jesus looked at Peter. Peter looked at Jesus. Jesus knew. Peter remembered. Compassion flowed from Jesus to Peter. Peter ran from Jesus into the dark. He had arrived at the entrance to the dark night of his soul.

Brave Enough to Think About It

1. *Unanswered questions, confusion, and devastating humiliation can all be part of discipleship.* The challenge is to be able to deal with them and keep on following. Again and again, Peter was told things he didn't understand. He was asked to do things that didn't make sense. He was told he was a tool of Satan and that he would be a deserter. Somehow, Peter found the fortitude to stay with Jesus. It's not the failings, but the strength of character and sheer faith that allow us to overcome the failings, that is the mark of a true disciple.

   a. What would make you stick around a leader who seemed to offer so much trouble? What would he have to offer to get you to stay?

   b. What unanswered questions do you have about following Jesus? What confusion does God's Word present for you? What makes you keep following despite the uncertainty?

   c. In what ways has following Jesus humiliated you? Have you ever been truly devastated by some aspect of your discipleship? How did you handle it?

2. *A humble attitude and a servant's spirit is crucial to true discipleship.* This lesson was so important — and so strongly disregarded by the disciples — that Jesus had to keep repeating it over and over again.

   a. Do you understand what Jesus means when He cautions us to have a servant's attitude? Explain how the concept plays out in your own life. When do you have a servant's attitude? When do you not?

   b. What menial tasks are you *not* willing to do? Why not? What would make you do them — not with a resentful attitude, but willingly?

   c. If you had been at the Passover with Jesus and the disciples, would you have volunteered to do the foot-washing? If so, what would motivate your service? If not, what would keep you from doing so?

3. *One of Satan's favorite tactics is to divide and conquer us so that we can't focus on the work of the Lord.* He often got the disciples to squabble among themselves about insignificant matters so that they couldn't concentrate on

the things Jesus was teaching them. We need to be on our guard and not allow the evil one to cause divisions between believers.

a. How does Satan divide and conquer in the church today? What examples of this have you seen in your local church body? What about in your family?

b. How can these internal divisions be prevented? What can you do to handle them once they've started?

c. In what ways has Satan distracted you from your purpose? How has he accomplished this? How can you put an end to it?

4. *Even in the midst of our unworthiness and failure, Jesus looks compassionately on us, offering mercy that we don't deserve. Accepting his benevolent mercy, we keep the door open for him to change us.* Peter's most devastating moment was when he realized he had, true to his Master's prediction, denied knowing him. Not only that, but Jesus had heard everything. Peter's sorrow, shame, and disgrace overwhelmed him. But Jesus' incredible love and compassion flowed toward Peter. This is the love that captures us, keeps us hanging on, and eventually transforms us.

a. When you are feeling unworthy, how do you relate to Jesus? What is it like to experience Christ's mercy and love when you're at your lowest?

b. Have you ever denied Christ outright? Are there passive ways you've denied him, such as being quiet about your faith when you should have spoken up? Which of your actions or behaviors have denied him? How have you dealt with this, if at all?

c. In the face of his disciples' clear unworthiness, Jesus prayed for them. Read his prayer (John 17:6-19). From this prayer, what do you conclude about the way Jesus prays for you now? Does it change anything about your faith to know that Jesus prays for you?

Brave Enough for Action

The idea of having a servant's heart was one of the most important lessons of Peter's life. It was also one of the most difficult for him to embrace. For so long, "humble" and "servant" remained mere words to Peter.

Assess where you are with respect to your own humble heart and servant's attitude. Are they still mere words?

Find out what it's like to be truly humble. Look around you and identify something that needs to be done — something you would never do. Maybe there's something in your home or family that your spouse normally takes care of or you hire somebody to do. Perhaps there's a job at your church that is so menial that no one wants to do it. You might see something in your work environment that someone "lower on the totem pole" usually handles. Pick something and do it — cheerfully and without telling anybody about it.

Why not make it a way of life? Every so often, just take out the trash. Refill the paper in the copy machine. Shovel the front steps of your church. Wash somebody's feet. Discover what Jesus was really talking about.

chapter 10

STRICKEN SHEPHERD, SCATTERED SHEEP

MATTHEW 27:32—28:10
MARK 15:21—16:14
LUKE 23:26—24:43
JOHN 19:17—21:23

s Jesus predicted, his disciples scattered as soon as He was arrested. Spirits were willing, but flesh was painfully weak. Peter had stubbornly refused to accept the possibility that he would collapse under pressure, but he had abandoned the cause like the rest of them, only more visibly. He who shouted loudest, fell hardest. He who'd bravely swung a sword in righteous indignation now sadly hung his head in agonizing shame.

It was just as Jesus had predicted. He knew Peter so well, and had seen the flaws in his character that made a downfall unsurprising. Hadn't Peter shown arrogant self-confidence when he contradicted the Lord, saying he'd never fail? Didn't he disparage his colleagues by suggesting that they — not he — might desert the Master? Hadn't he disregarded the reality of spiritual warfare? Satan had been trying to use him, but he was oblivious. Peter's rebuke of Jesus was motivated by the Prince of Darkness, but he failed to recognize it.

Then there was the serious issue of his lack of spiritual discipline. Granted, he was exhausted in the garden of Gethsemane, but so was Jesus and He didn't fall asleep. But Peter's failure to "watch and pray" when specifically told to meant that he layed himself open to Satan's temptation and robbed himself of the necessary armor to counter it. Add all these factors together, and his collapse was eminently predictable.

While Peter disappeared from the scene, Jesus was thrust onto center stage. Brought bound before the Jewish religious elite who interrogated him relentlessly, Jesus steadfastly stood by his claim to be the Son of God. In the ears of his hearers, this was blasphemy, a capital offense. They were determined Jesus must die. They not only wanted him dead, they wanted him hanged on a tree — for this would show him to be cursed by God and negate any claims to Messiah-ship (see Deuteronomy 21:23). But only the Roman authorities could pass a death sentence and implement the execution. So they took Jesus to Pontius Pilate, the Roman governor who was in residence in Jerusalem at the time.

Pilate, sitting in judgment of Jesus, showed himself to be more of a politician than a judge. After a lengthy discussion with Jesus, Pilate could find no reason to execute him. In fact, Jesus seemed to be more concerned about Pilate's eternal well-being than his own critical situation. But Pilate, throwing legal concerns to the wind, caved in to political threats and fickle public demands and ordered Jesus flogged. After much shouting by the Jews, he handed Jesus over to them to be crucified. Peter was missing throughout all of these dark events.

The crucifixion was carried out in front of crowds of witnesses, some cheering, others horrified and mourning. Jesus, looking down into the multitude from the cross, saw his mother and the young disciple John standing together. How painful it must have been not to see Peter beside them. John's presence made Peter's absence all the more glaring. Jesus asked John to take care of his mother, which John did for the rest of Mary's days.

When it was all over, apparently the twelve apostles were nowhere to be found. Perhaps John had taken Mary home to spare her any more agony. It fell to some relatively unknown and courageous followers of Jesus, Nicodemus and Joseph of Arimathea, to claim the body of Jesus from the authorities, take it down from the cross, and give him a respectable burial. And it fell to a small group of women disciples to mark the place where the body was laid to rest.

Somewhere in the vicinity of Jerusalem, Peter was in hiding. The city was full of the news of Jesus' crucifixion, and no doubt Peter heard the details and sank further into a dark hole of sorrow, questions, bitter recrimination, and self-pity. He was a broken man. Repeatedly, the Master had talked about the fact that He was going to die, and Peter had refused to listen. Each time He'd mentioned his death, He had revealed there would be a resurrection. Peter had a mental block on that issue, too.

Now was the time Peter needed to remember what he'd been taught, but he was in a fog. His closed mind had erected a formidable barrier to the truth. If he had truly heard what he'd been told, he would have been scouring Jerusalem for signs of a living Christ, who had triumphed over death and hell. He would have been in energized anticipation instead of wallowing in a pit of despair. Peter was dying a thousand deaths and living in a hell of his own making.

But Jesus had not finished with Peter. So when He rose from the dead, He left word with the angelic messenger that news of his resurrection should be given to Peter in particular. Peter, more than any of them, needed the good news. In spite of the magnitude of Peter's recent failings, Jesus had nothing but love and compassion for him.

Somebody found Peter and brought him to the place where the other scattered sheep had slowly reassembled. To say that there was tension in the room among that group of men would be an understatement. They were conscious of their failure to stand by the Lord despite their insistence that they would. Some of the disciples were in outright denial, acting as if nothing of significance had happened. Some were emotionally overwrought, incapable of looking their brothers in the eyes. Some wanted to talk; others wanted to be left alone. This was a group of men in total disarray. The sheep, without their shepherd, were a forlorn bunch.

Suddenly there was an urgent knock on the heavily barred door, and the sound of women's voices, high-pitched with urgency. Quickly they were admitted and the doors firmly secured again. Breathless, the women began to pour out an incredible story. They had gone to the tomb where the body of Jesus had been laid, but on arrival had found the guard gone, the seal broken, the heavy stone rolled away, and the tomb utterly empty.

"Someone stole the body," muttered one of the men.

"Must be the guards. But why?" exclaimed another.

"The religious leaders did it. They don't want the tomb to become a shrine," pronounced a third.

"No, no, please listen to us," cried the women.

Reluctantly, the men turned their attention to them. What did these women know about military matters and political issues?

"There's more. We saw an angel . . ."

"A what?" the men chorused.

"An angel. He said that Jesus has risen. That He is alive and we should not be looking for the living among the dead, and that we were to come and tell you."

"Enough already. Nonsense!" grumbled a male voice.

But Peter looked closely at the women, and there was something about their composure that struck him. *Why are they so excited, while we're so miserable?* He was intrigued. So with his friend John, he got further details from the women, quietly left the room, and together they ran to the tomb. They saw that the women's words were true. There were the empty tomb and the grave clothes, but no body. Peter was perplexed. If the body had been stolen, why had it first been unwrapped from its burial clothes? And why were the burial clothes so carefully arranged, as if the body were still inside? *It doesn't add up.* Even after his death, Jesus was still confounding Peter.

Later that evening, the disciples were gathered together, wondering what to do. By this time Judas was no more. Overwhelmed by guilt and shame, he had taken his own life. Thomas was nowhere to be seen. The disciples wondered about his well-being because of his melancholic temperament. *Where was he? Had he fallen apart?* So that left ten of them, standing around, morose, lost, directionless. Suddenly, without warning, Jesus stood in the middle of the group.

Talk about emotional overload. Terror, incredulity, joy, embarrassment — all at the same time. It was more than the human mind was designed to handle. But Jesus was totally at ease and calmly and quietly greeted them almost formally. "Peace be with you," He said with a smile. As He stretched out his hands in customary greeting, they saw the ugly scars from the crucifixion nails.

Some rushed to embrace him. Others, more reticent, held back. He winced as the men enthusiastically hugged him with strong fisherman's arms. Stepping back, He showed them why. His rib cage was bruised, his side deeply scarred, the flesh cruelly torn. In their excitement at seeing him alive, they had forgotten He had recently been dead.

But now He was very much alive and ready to do business. He reminded them of their calling and the commission that He had given them. They were to be involved in announcing the forgiveness of sins. He repeated his teaching that He had been sent into the world on a mission, and that it was now their turn to be sent out as missionaries, too. The promised Holy Spirit would shortly empower them. *There's that "Holy Spirit" thing again. What's He talking about?* Jesus breathed on the men, demonstrating how the Father would breathe out the Spirit, and they would inhale his empowering "grace by faith." Then, as suddenly and effortlessly as He had arrived, He was gone.

During the next few days Jesus visited them again. Thomas was there, and he saw for himself the incontrovertible evidence that Jesus was alive. Slowly, the disciples adjusted to the knowledge that Jesus had truly risen from the dead, but they were still mystified about his plans. He kept saying He was leaving, and each time He went, they wondered if they would see him again. But He had promised to come back for them, and each time He returned, they wondered if next time He left, they'd go with him. Then there was the matter of the empowering of the Holy Spirit. He had told them not to leave the city until the Spirit was poured out upon them. But they weren't at all sure how this would happen or what to expect. To add to their confusion, Jesus said He'd meet them in Galilee.

The thought of returning to the familiar surroundings of Galilee was appealing. Their time in Jerusalem had been traumatic, and it would feel good to be home. They were still unsure if they were in danger of arrest, although the authorities seemed to be preoccupied denying reports of Jesus' appearances throughout the city. It was the topic of conversation everywhere.

So the men left the city as inconspicuously as possible. As they retraced their steps, they passed many familiar sites where Jesus had performed a miracle or told them something memorable. They reminisced with each other about all that had happened. It had only been a few weeks before, but it seemed like another lifetime. They wondered how they would survive without him. *What exactly does He want us to do?*

They talked about the three years they had watched Jesus in

action. They smiled, remembering the exhilaration, shook their heads at the staggering humiliations. Mile after hot, dusty mile they had followed him, sometimes rushing ahead, often lagging far behind. But their experience had now been taken to a new level, and they were trying to digest it. *The Resurrection.*

Their natural skepticism had insulated them against any acceptance of Jesus' predictions that He would be crucified and rise again. But the events that had unfolded before their eyes now required them to reconsider, and in doing so, they found themselves facing many daunting questions about the Master. They had seen him triumph over disease, calm storms, read their motives, cast out demonic powers, raise the dead, feed the multitudes, and teach the Scriptures. They had learned to adjust to each new startling revelation, but this latest was the most difficult. He had died, been buried, and on the third day had risen from the dead.

During the conversation, someone mentioned the puzzling statement of John the Baptist years ago when he'd introduced them to Jesus. He'd said, "Behold the Lamb of God who takes away the sin of the world." They recounted the way Jesus had eaten the Passover lamb and had said something about the bread being his broken body and the wine his shed blood. His body had been cruelly broken, his blood mercilessly shed. Was He saying that his death was the fulfillment of the symbolism of Passover? Was his resurrection a divine assurance that his sacrifice was indeed sufficient to take away the sins of the world? In rising from the dead, was He showing that death held no terrors for him, and should not hold any for them either if they devoted themselves to him and his cause? The road to Galilee was long, and they had plenty of time to wrestle with these and a thousand other questions. Peter, uncharacteristically subdued, kept his thoughts to himself. He had said enough over the years. Now a little silence and a lot of reflection were in order.

It would be some time before they could begin to put all the pieces together, and that was going to require the aid of the Holy Spirit anyway. The one thing they could grasp was that now they could see a ray of hope. Jesus had risen from the dead and come back to them. Utter failures though they were, Jesus, in the moment of his greatest triumph — the greatest victory known to humanity — had come back to them. He understood; He hadn't given up on them. Even though He had gone away, He promised to come back and promised to send his Spirit. They clung tightly to their new hope — hope for what, they weren't sure.

A few days later they were home again, and what stories they had to tell! The big question was when the Master would appear. They had no doubts that He would. Meanwhile, they each settled back into their old routines. They never strayed far from each other. These sheep had scattered, but now they were together again.

The other disciples were not sure how to treat Peter. He was such a forceful presence in the group, but his shameful behavior had seriously undermined his credibility. His mighty ego had taken a severe blow, so he was laying low. The group was feeling uneasy with Jesus out of the picture and Peter seemingly out of energy. They felt like a rudderless boat in a rough sea.

Back at the lakeside with his family and his boats, Peter one day announced, "I'm going fishing." He needed to be back where he was comfortable — at home on the water with his nets.

Six of the other men decided to go with him, and late in the evening they set sail. As the night wore on, their enthusiasm wore off. The fish weren't there. When the dark of night gradually gave way to the gentle break of dawn, the cold and hungry group headed for shore. There was a chilling mist hanging low over the water, and as they approached the beach they could see a fire burning. A voice echoed over the still surface of the lake, "Hey guys, you didn't catch anything, did you?" They didn't need reminding. "Not tonight."

"Try casting one more time on the right side of the boat."

Perhaps from his vantage point, the man could see something. It was worth trying. So the nets were hoisted over the side, and the fish appeared as if by magic. In a matter of moments, they had a net-breaking catch. How could they not make the connection? *Déjà vu,* big time. The voice, the fish, and the memory of a similar event on the same lake years before. "It's the Lord!" John shouted.

Peter, his old self again, leaped over the side of the boat and began swimming mightily, as fast as he could, the last hundred yards to shore. Coughing and sputtering, he arrived just before his more sedate companions on the boat. He staggered onto the beach, breathless, and just stood there, looking at his Master. Jesus smiled at Peter's childlike enthusiasm. This was the Peter He loved. The one He had chosen. Broken — yet still here.

Jesus had breakfast cooking on the fire. He instructed the men to bring their catch ashore. As Peter pulled in the net and counted the fish — customary because the men divided the catch — he noted they had 153 big ones. And the net was still intact.

Peter, dripping and shivering in the cool morning, wrapped his cloak around him and sat by the fire. Breakfast was served. The Lord waited on the disciples, who ate in silence, once more overcome by the calm, strong majesty of his presence.

Jesus spoke into the stillness. "Simon son of John, do you truly love me more than these?" He asked in front of the group. Peter was startled. The formal address, "Simon son of John," was unusual. *Is Jesus angry with me?* Maybe He was trying to ensure that Peter caught the solemnity of the question. *But what exactly is He asking? Do you love me more than you love these men? Or did He mean, do you love me more than you love these things — the boats and lake and fishing? Or did He mean, Simon, do you love me more than these men love me?*

Peter felt as if he was in the water over his head. All he could answer was, "Yes, Lord you know that I love you." Breathing a relieved sigh, Peter hoped that Jesus would be satisfied with his answer. Jesus then told him, "Feed my lambs."

Peter looked quizzically at Jesus, but the Master wasn't finished. He repeated his question, this time dropping any hint of comparison. "Simon son of John, do you truly love me?" He asked, looking directly at the uncomfortable disciple. Peter's response was exactly the same as his former reply. Jesus said, "Take care of my sheep." This was excruciating. Such scrutiny in front of his companions. Hadn't he been humiliated enough?

Apparently not. Jesus, for the third time, inquired about Peter's love for him. Deeply troubled by the questioning and still smarting from his own guilt and shame, Peter blurted out, "Lord, you know all things; you know that I love you." He was right. The Lord did know all things. He had shown the men repeatedly that He did not need anyone to tell him what was in a man. He knew that Peter loved him, and He was well aware of the deficiencies in his love. *So why is He putting me through the embarrassment?*

As Peter looked away from the Master's gaze, he noted the charcoal fire was burning low, and his mind leaped back to another small fire in the High Priest's courtyard. There he'd been asked three questions by three different people, and he had responded three times with denials, oaths, and curses. His darkest night. Were the three questions by this fire coincidental, or was the Master carefully giving him an opportunity to retract his three denials with affirmations of love?

And what had the Master just said to him? Something about feeding and shepherding his sheep and caring for his lambs. Was the Master publicly reaffirming his calling? Had He interrogated Peter in front of his friends to affirm him, rather than to embarrass him?

Any doubts Peter may have had were soon dispelled. Taking him to one side, Jesus told him, "Just keep on following." That was the signal. He was not being banished; he had not been terminated. Jesus was making it as simple as He possibly could. He had questioned Peter about his love and had instructed Peter about following. This was the key. It was all about loving and following.

Following meant following when he didn't want to, didn't think he could, didn't understand where he was going, didn't like what he was seeing, didn't feel like sacrificing any more. But now Peter had an example. Jesus had followed through, even to the point of death on a cross. Peter had tried to stop him, but Jesus would not be deterred. Peter's resolve to "keep on following" would have to be just as strong. Peter would learn to please the Lord, even when his actions would not necessarily please other people.

Jesus told Peter that the time would come — when he was old — that he would be led away, his arms stretched out, to somewhere he didn't want to go. Peter got the message. He was being warned in advance that he would have a long life in the Lord's service that would end in martyrdom. That was good news and bad news. He didn't relish the thought of martyrdom — only masochists do. But he did like the sound of a long life in the service of the Lord he loved.

Amazingly, right after letting Peter know that he would die in a way that would glorify God, Jesus repeated, "Follow me!" How scary. How profound. Jesus had been martyred on the cross to glorify God, and He was telling Peter to follow him. Unto death? *Gladly*. On a cross? *I'm not worthy*.

Tradition tells us that some three decades later, at the end of a life of dedicated service to the Lord, Peter was indeed crucified — martyred for his faith. But by this time he was a completely different person. He was humility personified. He thought himself unworthy to die in the same way as Jesus Christ, his Lord and Master, and so at his own request, was crucified head-downward.

192 BRAVE ENOUGH to FOLLOW

But right at this moment, Peter was encouraged. He was back where he belonged. Sadder, but infinitely wiser. For he had seen the Lord in a new light — more loving than he dared hope, more powerful than he'd imagined, more determined than he'd seen him before.

Peter glanced around with new eyes and new optimism and saw — he saw John. John the youngster, who had always had a special place in the Master's affections. At times it had troubled Peter. When they had started out together with Jesus, John had been so like Peter. Tempestuous, opinionated, difficult. But over time, there had been a remarkable mellowing in John. Peter knew it, and it added to his own sense of insecurity. He wondered if John had been listening to this very private conversation. "What about him?" Peter asked, pointing in John's direction. *How's John going to die?*

Jesus smiled. This was so like Peter. One moment moving easily in the realm of great spiritual matters, the next hitting earth with a bump. "Peter," He said patiently, "That's no concern of yours. If I want him to remain alive until I return, what is that to you? You must follow me."

For the last time, Jesus was telling Peter not to compare himself with others. The only important thing was to keep following.

For many years, that is precisely what Peter did. His transformation was remarkable. By the time he sat down to write the letters that appear in the Bible as 1 and 2 Peter, he had gone from brash and untamed to gentle yet as strong-willed as ever. True to Jesus' instructions, he had spent his life feeding the Master's sheep. Words like "humble" and "submit" were favorites in his vocabulary. Where once he'd vigorously protested the idea of Christ's death, in the end he commended Christ's suffering as an ideal. He truly became a Rock, and the church to this day honors his memory.

Rightly so, for he taught us many things. It doesn't matter how unlikely a follower you are. It doesn't matter if you're not cut out to be a leader. It doesn't matter if you don't know what you're supposed to do. Just love the Lord and keep on following. In the power of the Holy Spirit, you will profoundly influence the world for good, and Jesus will recognize you as one who loves him, one who is brave enough to follow.

BRAVE ENOUGH TO THINK ABOUT IT

1. *If it could happen to Peter, it could happen to anyone.* Jesus had predicted Peter's moral and spiritual downfall. Peter crashed and burned in full view of his best friends and everyone throughout history ever since. Why does Scripture emphasize Peter's failure? Why couldn't we graciously overlook his weaknesses and highlight his strengths? It's a warning to all of us — if the Rock can shake, so can we.

    a. What are some things about Peter's attitude and behavior that made his downfall predictable? What can you identify in your own life that is similar?

    b. Can you identify times in your life when you've hidden from the Lord, as Peter did during the events surrounding the Crucifixion? What caused you to do this? Have you come out of hiding, and if so, what brought you out?

    c. Have you ever had what you considered to be a spiritual downfall? How did you handle it? How did Jesus communicate with you? If this has never happened to you, what do you think could cause it?

2. *Despite our failure, we will never be abandoned by the Master.* Peter's desertion of Jesus was complete. He was nowhere to be seen during the trial, Crucifixion, and burial. Yet Christ's compassion for Peter's tormented soul was so great that He sent word through the angel, mentioning Peter by name, that He would meet the disciples in Galilee. In the face of their rejection, Jesus was still pursuing the hearts of his men.

    a. Have you ever had the sense of Christ pursuing you through your own dark times? How did this strike you? How did you respond?

    b. How easy or difficult is it for you to believe that you really won't be abandoned by Christ? What circumstances in your life cause you to think you might anger him so much that He throws in the towel?

    c. Knowing that Christ's love is unconditional, have you ever adopted a *laissez faire* attitude about your behavior? Have you ever shrugged your shoulders at your own failures, saying, "I'm only human. . . . God will forgive me." What is the danger of this mind-set?

3. *When we have been broken by our own failure, the knowledge of the risen Christ makes all the difference, turning defeat into triumph and shame into glory.* Peter was in hiding because he thought it was all over and he'd lost. His defeat began to turn to triumph when he finally realized that Jesus had actually risen — just as He'd predicted. Christ had truly conquered death — and that meant He could conquer anything. We can't live in defeat and shame, because Christ has risen! This is what Christianity is all about.

   a. How does the knowledge of the risen Christ make a difference in your life?

   b. Are there times when the words "Christ has risen" seem like mere words? What makes the difference between the words and the true meaning that pierces your heart?

   c. What's wrong with focusing on your guilt and shame, knowing that Christ has risen?

4. *Jesus wants us to keep on following.* Despite our problems, doubts, and failures, He loves us. He knows that we love him. And He instructs us to follow. He made this abundantly clear to Peter. Christ's final words to Peter in the Gospels are, "Follow me!" An insistent, urgent command, meant for all of us. As long as we keep following him, He'll keep working on us.

   a. What are your obstacles to following Jesus? What are some obstacles you might encounter in the future?

   b. What have you learned that can help you follow even when you don't want to?

   c. What kind of work are you hoping Jesus will do in you? What are some things He did for Peter that you wish He'd do for you?

196 BRAVE ENOUGH *to* FOLLOW

BRAVE ENOUGH FOR ACTION

Now might be a good time for a serious assessment of your own attitudes and behaviors to determine whether you're safe from a spiritual downfall like Peter's or whether you're headed down the slippery slope toward one.

A collapse such as Peter's doesn't happen overnight. Usually, a major failure is the culmination of a series of actions and attitudes. Use the following list of Peter's contributing factors to help you evaluate your own situation.

· *Personality flaws.* Every personality strength has a flip side. Peter's commendable willingness to take a lead meant that he was inclined to reckless words and impetuous actions. Wise followers know themselves inside out and guard against their inbuilt flaws. Peter didn't.

· *Arrogant attitudes.* Peter had good reason to believe that he was a privileged person who had been granted a position of great significance. But he did not handle this well. He became inordinately self-confident, as if he had forgotten that he was made by Jesus.

· *Relational difficulties.* Peter's outspoken lack of confidence in his fellow apostles' commitment showed he had not yet learned to avoid petty jealousies, comparisons, and putting others down to lift himself up. His relationships with his fellow apostles suffered because of it.

· *Lack of spiritual discipline.* More than once, Jesus had reminded Peter of the place of prayer in the life of the follower, culminating in the sad scene in Gethsemane where he fell asleep though specifically commissioned to watch and pray. Carelessness in spiritual discipline leaves the disciple vulnerable to spiritual attack.

· *Selective belief.* Peter's well-documented distaste for being told what to do meant that he tended to listen to what he wanted to hear and accept what he was ready to believe. This leads to a belief system based on a dangerous mix of truth and error.

· *Ignorance of spiritual dynamics.* On more than one occasion, Jesus found it necessary to point out Satan's activity. Peter was apparently blissfully unaware of it, but a disciple can't afford to be unaware of the true dynamic of spiritual warfare.

· *Unresolved feelings of inadequacy.* No one reading the account of Peter's single-handed defense of Jesus in Gethsemane could ever accuse him of cowardice. But at the same time, he failed to speak up in the High Priest's courtyard and lied about his allegiance to Jesus. Apparently he felt confident he could do something with his fists but was unnerved by fear and feelings of inadequacy when required to move out of familiar territory. There was no doubt his spirit was willing. The problem was his flesh was weak.

Do you have anything in common with Peter? If you find some areas of concern, begin to pray about them, and determine what action you might take to turn them around.

For three years Peter had been with Jesus. What a relationship! For three glorious, dreadful years they scaled the heights and plumbed the depths. The highs were breathtaking, the lows mind-numbing. Through it all, Jesus remained constant and committed. He showed He believed in Peter and was committed to his well-being. From the beginning, Jesus envisioned the fisherman as the Rock, and He never changed his mind.

Despite his many failings and well documented weaknesses, Peter continued to follow. That's what he was told to do. That's what he did. Therein lies the secret of this unlikely leader. Right from the beginning, it was all about Peter following and Jesus making. "Follow me, and I will make you fishers of men," Jesus said back when the great adventure began. Three years later, you could see the results.

In the process of following the Master, Peter had witnessed a thousand wonders and learned a host of lessons. But two big ones stood out: the reality of who Jesus is and the truth about himself. Not that he'd learned everything there is to know about the Master — no one ever does this side of glory. Neither had he been transformed into a polished disciple. But he had learned that Jesus is the Risen Lord, and that he was the Lord's humble servant. He knew that Jesus is the Truth — about God and man and life itself, and he knew better than to go looking for reality anywhere else.

From here on out, it was going to be a matter of following the Master the way he'd learned — but with one big difference. The Master would no longer be visibly and tangibly present, striding alongside in the body of a vigorous young man. He would be residing within Peter in the person of the Holy Spirit, whose imminent arrival Peter had learned to anticipate and in whose power Peter was poised to operate. Same Peter, same Jesus, same principles. He had to keep on doing what he'd been taught, empowered by the Spirit within him, and Jesus would keep on making him what He wanted him to be.

And that's how it is for all God's people. We are called to be with Jesus in the ups and downs of daily life. Indwelt by his Spirit, enriched by his Word, empowered and guided, rebuked and corrected. We, too, can anticipate being changed slowly and imperceptibly into the people He wants us to be.

The story of Peter, of course, is far from over. But we've seen him through the most formative time of his life, the time in which he went from fisherman to Rock, the time when he finally became brave enough to follow. Here we'll leave him, for now. Peter would go on to be one of the greatest evangelists of all time, helping to build Christ's early church. He became the leader Jesus had been grooming him to be, and you can read about it in the book of Acts. He still wasn't perfect. He was still Peter. He was still a most unlikely leader, but he kept on following.

What advice would Peter leave with us? He ended his second letter with the words, "But grow in the grace and knowledge of our

Lord and Savior Jesus Christ. To him be glory both now and forever! Amen" (2 Peter 3:18). I think he's telling us that in order to realize our divinely imparted potential and become what we were created to be, we just need to keep on following. That the key to life, love, and leadership is simply, "Just keep on loving and following Jesus, and He'll keep on making you what He wants you to be."

At the end of his life, Simon Peter was martyred for his faith. Finally, he made it into heaven for a grand reunion with the One he'd been with for three years and followed for many more. Now they could spend eternity together. And one day, all the rest of us who are brave enough to follow will join them.

NOTES

1. Charles Haddon Spurgeon, quoted from Greatest
   Quotations.com. Website: http://www.greatest
   quotations.com/search.asp?quote=Enemies&page=3.
   Accessed September 13, 2003.

ABOUT THE AUTHOR

Stuart Briscoe was born in Millom, Cumbria, England in 1930. At the age of seventeen he embarked on a career in banking and simultaneously started to preach, and for twelve years these two occupations filled his time.

In 1959, Stuart and his wife, Jill, left the business world to share in the ministry of the Torchbearers, a youth organization reaching out to the far corners of the globe. During the next several years, Stuart and Jill raised three children — David, Judy, and Peter — and traveled extensively.

In 1970, Stuart became pastor of Elmbrook Church in Brookfield, Wisconsin. Since then, the church has grown to a weekly attendance of more than 7,000, and has planted eight sister churches in the Milwaukee area. Elmbrook's TV and radio ministries, *Telling the Truth*, feature Stuart and Jill and are broadcast widely. After thirty years as Senior Pastor at Elmbrook Church, Stuart has stepped down, and he and Jill are now ministers-at-large on Elmbrook's staff.

God has blessed Stuart and Jill with thirteen grandchildren at last count. Stuart has ministered in more than one hundred countries, and in his spare time he likes to read, run (not at the same time), garden, and enjoy God's creation.